A WEST COAST CHRISTMAS

A WEST COAST CHRISTMAS

Celebrating the Season
on the Edge of the Pacific

Edited by Anne Tempelman-Kluit

WHITECAP BOOKS
VANCOUVER/TORONTO

The information contained in this book is true and complete to the best of our knowledge. All recommendations are made without guarantee on the part of the editor or Whitecap Books Ltd. The editor and publisher disclaim any liability in connection with the use of this information. For additional information please contact Whitecap Books Ltd., 351 Lynn Avenue, North Vancouver, BC, V7J 2C4.

Every effort has been taken to trace the ownership of copyright material used in the text. The editor and publisher welcome any information enabling them to rectify any reference or credit in subsequent editions.

Copy-edited by Elizabeth McLean
Cover and interior design by Warren Clark
Cover illustration by Ted Harrison
Interior illustrations by Andrew Costen and Nadaleen Tempelman-Kluit

Printed in Canada

Canadian Cataloguing in Publication Data
A West Coast christmas

 ISBN 1-55110-956-5

 1. Christmas—Northwest, Pacific—Literary collections.
2. Christmas—Alaska—Literary collections. 3. American literature—20th century.
4. Canadian literature (English)—20th century.*
I. Tempelman-Kluit, Anne, 1941–
GT4987.05W47 1999   810.8'0334   C99-910848-4

The publisher acknowledges the support of the Canada Council for the Arts for our publishing program and the Cultural Services Branch of the Government of British Columbia in making this publication possible. We acknowledge the financial support of the Government of Canada through the Book Industry Development Program for our publishing activities.

For more information on other titles from Whitecap Books, visit our web site at www.whitecap.ca

For Annemarie and Nadaleen

and those exceptional Christmas Stockings.

Acknowledgments

The nicest thing about researching a book such as this one is how many interesting and interested people you meet. The librarians, especially Wendy Godley and Melina Bowden in Special Collections at the Vancouver Public Library, Doreen Stephens at the Anglican Church Archives, Bob Stewart at the United Church Archives, Kathleen Neece and Karly Tucker at the Lummi Island Library, all gave generous help. Archivists at the Vancouver Maritime Museum, the Vancouver Museum, the Seattle Museum of History and Industry, and Craigdarroch Castle in Victoria patiently unearthed clues and photographs. Sandra Parrish at the Campbell River Museum dug up cards literally overnight. Grania McWhirter and Marina never gave up, Andrew Costen and Nadaleen conjured up drawings, Annemarie performed small miracles of detection. Dirk fought and was almost conquered by a computer virus. To all of you, and many others, my thanks.

Contents

Foreword by Rick Hansen

I've lived on the West Coast for most of my life and I will always cherish my Christmas memories. For me, *A West Coast Christmas* is truly about family, friends, togetherness and love.

My two most memorable Christmas stories are very different from each other but they share similar values. Christmas 1986 was during my Man in Motion World Tour. After almost two years on the road, I was finally back in Canada. Unfortunately, it was during the dead of winter. If you've ever tried to wheel or ride a bike in the snow, you will understand how challenging it was. On December 23, I woke up feeling so sick that I had to see a doctor. He ordered me to rest immediately. At first, I was disappointed because I had plans to spend Christmas with my fiancée Amanda. But then I tried to put things in perspective. I was on the homeward leg of my journey, I was surrounded by people I cared about and who cared for me. It's amazing how a shift in perspective can change how you feel. My crew and I checked into a log cabin motel, brought in an evergreen tree and shared all kinds of presents. It ended up being a wonderful time because it focused on friends and sharing—the important things of Christmas.

My other favourite holiday memory was in 1992 when our eldest daughter, Emma, first understood what all the Christmas excitement was about. Emma was almost three years old and she started to make the connection between our preparations and the story of Santa, Rudolph and the elves. I will never forget seeing her doubtful expression as she listened to our explanation on Christmas Eve of what would happen to her stocking that night. Needless to say, she was skeptical. The look on her face the next morning when she saw that Santa had indeed made a visit was priceless. The joy and excitement in a child's eyes at the wonder of it all captures the spirit of Christmas for me.

Introduction

Christmas has many voices. Happy, pensive, excited, wistful: how people tell their stories reflects attitudes, moods and customs of their times. Some sentiments of the season are foreign to us now, some festive customs archaic, but Christmas continues to be the focus of winter for most people on the West Coast.

While researching a book about Christmas in the Klondike two years ago, I came across many stories from the West Coast. I was intrigued that, despite differences in time and place, many of these tales shared a common theme of isolation and little money, coupled with the determination to celebrate the holiday wherever they were, and however poor their prospects.

One problem with researching a subject such as Christmas is knowing when to stop. Like a Christmas garland, one thing leads to another and the next link is always too promising to ignore. My family are convinced there will be "Christmas" books for the next ten years. My inclination to rummage through the early-day lives of others is, happily, well supported by a wealth of material in archives, libraries and museums. Events of this special day are chronicled in many letters, journals, diaries, newspapers and reminiscences—published and unpublished.

I discovered West Coast Christmas tales of comfortable lives in blooming new cities, with loving, affluent families. But more often, Christmas memories involved hardship and isolation. I was reminded again of the hardships people

accepted as simply part of life; told with humour and, from today's perspective, an amazing matter-of-factness. People embarked on long journeys, mostly by sea, often in uncertain weather, to keep Christmas with their "neighbours," sometimes the first people they had seen in months. Money was scarce, but people were generous. Christmas dinners were a community effort, and turkey was a rare treat, but someone usually managed to produce a duck, or catch a fish. Christmas trees grew outside the door and decorations could be improvised from pages of a catalogue or even from overwintering berries.

The recipes in this book come from many sources. The Clatsop County Plum Pudding is sold each year at Christmas events to raise funds for the Historical Society. Every year we make the Christmas cake that came from an Australian friend's mother at least twenty years ago. Pound Cake and Steamed Pudding came from my mother. An Empress Hotel chef contributed the Scrumpy. I have never been ambitious enough to cook a Christmas goose, but this recipe, again from a friend, sounds wonderful. Most of us have our own special Christmas treats, something else that sets this holiday apart.

The Christmas cards featured here are from early days. Then, cards commonly pictured flowers and bluebells, or were lacy confections now more fitting for Valentine's Day than Christmas. Later came holly and snow scenes.

Isolated from the rest of the continent by the Rocky Mountains, the West Coast is naturally distinctive. It has given a common history to people from Alaska to Oregon, and attitudes and lifestyles disregard borders. Indeed, when many of these stories were written, there were no borders. My initial idea of a book focusing on Christmas celebrations along the British Columbia coast soon expanded to embrace neighbouring states.

I don't recall many white Christmases in Vancouver over the past thirty years, but those we have had only made a special time more special. I do remember many rainy Christmas afternoons walking our dogs on the beach, and thinking ahead to being by the fire, curtains drawn, with family and friends. The greyness outside actually enhanced the warmth inside. And listening to the voices in this book, it would take a lot more than weather to dampen the Christmas spirit.

These stories are our history.

December 24th

by Hubert Evans
Roberts Creek, B.C.

I miss the sleigh bells and the sparkling snow
which marked this season long ago.
But now my heart is gladdened
for beyond the reef I see
a passing ship and through the rain
its masthead Christmas Tree.

All decked out for Christmas.

From Whittlings

Hubert Evans was a prolific writer of short stories, plays and books, who began writing poetry when he was eighty-three. He built a house in Roberts Creek in 1920, where he raised his family and had a wonderful garden. Hubert Evans died in 1986.

Victoria Christmas

by Emily Carr
Victoria, B.C., circa 1885

Victoria Christmas weather was always nippy—generally there was snow. We sewed presents for weeks before Christmas came—kettle holders, needle books, pen wipers and cross-stitch bookmarkers. Just before Christmas we went out into the woods, cut down a fir tree and brought it home so alive still that the warm house fooled it into thinking spring had come, and it breathed delicious live pine smell all over the house. We put fir and holly behind all the pictures and on the mantlepiece and everywhere.

Plum puddings were dangling from under the pantry shelf by the tails of their boiling cloths. A month ago, we had all sat round the breakfast-room table, stoning raisins while someone read a story aloud. Everyone had given the pudding a good-luck stir before it went into the bowls and was tied down and boiled for hours in the copper wash boiler while spicy smells ran all over the house. On Christmas Day the biggest pudding came out for a final boil before being brought to the table with brandy fire leaping up its sides from the dish, and with a sprig of holly scorching and crackling on its top.

A Merry Xmas from a Victorian-era child in Victoria.

4

Christmas Eve Father took us into town to see the shops lit up. Every lamp post had a fir tree tied to it—not corpsy old trees but fresh cut firs. Victoria streets were dark; this made the shops look all the brighter. Windows were decorated with mock snow made of cotton wool and diamond dust. Drygoods shops did not have much that was Christmassy to display except red flannel and rabbit fur baby coats and muffs and tippets. Chemists had immense globes of red, green and blue medicine hanging from brass chains in their shop windows. I wished some of us could be sick enough for Dr. Helmcken to prescribe one of the splendid globes for us. The chemists also showed coloured soap and fancy perfume in bottles. Castor oil in hideous blue bottles peered from behind nice Christmas things and threw out hints about over-eating and stomach-ache. A horrid woman once told my mother that she let her children eat everything they wanted on Christmas Day and finished them up with a big dose of castor oil. Mr. Hibben, the stationer, was nicer than that woman and the chemist. He hid all the school books behind story books left open at the best pictures. He had "Merry Christmas" in cotton wool on red cardboard in his window.

It was the food shops that Merry Christmassed the hardest. In Mr. Saunders', the grocer's, window was a real Santa Claus grinding coffee. The wheel was bigger than he was. He had a long beard and moved his hands and his head. As the wheel went round the coffee beans went in, got ground, and came out, smell and all. In the window all round Santa were bonbons, cluster raisins, nuts and candied fruit, besides long walking-sticks made of peppermint candy. Next to this splendid window came Goodacre's horrible butcher shop—

everything in it dead and naked. Dead geese and turkeys waggled, head down; dead beeves, calves and pigs straddled between immense meat hooks on the walls; naked sheep had bunches of coloured paper where their heads ought to have been and flowers and squiggles carved in the fat on their backs. Creatures that still had their heads on stared out of eyes like poached eggs when the white has run over the yolk. Baby pigs looked worst of all—pink and naked as bathing babies, their cheeks drawn back to make them smile at the red apples which had been forced into their toothless, sucking mouths. The shop floor was strewn deep in sawdust to catch blood drips. You heard no footsteps in the shop, only the sharpening of knives, sawing of bones, and bump, bump of the scale. Everybody was examining meat and saying, "Compliments of the Season" to everyone else, Father saying, "Fine display, Goodacre, very fine indeed!" We children rushed out and went back to Santa while Father chose his meat.

The shop of old George, the poulterer, was nearly as bad as Goodacre's, only the dead things did not look so dead, nor stare so hard, having shut the grey lids over their eyes to die. They were limp in necks and stiff in legs. As most of them had feathers on they looked like birds still, whereas the butcher's creatures had been rushed at once from life to meat.

The food shops ended the town, and after that came Johnson Street and Chinatown, which was full of black night. Here we turned back towards James' Bay, ready for bed.

There was a high mantlepiece in the breakfast room. And while we were hanging our stockings from it my sister read:

Twas the night before Christmas and all through the house
Not a creature was stirring, not even a mouse.

On the way to bed we could smell our Christmas tree waiting in the dining-room. The room was all dark but we knew that it stood on the floor and touched the ceiling and that it hung heavy with presents, ready for to-morrow. When the lights were lit there would be more of them than any of us children could count. We would all take hands and sing carols round the tree; Bong would come in and look with his mouth open. There was always things on it for him but he would not wait to get his presents. He would run back to his kitchen and we would take them to him there. It seemed as if Bong felt too Chinese to Christmas with us in our Canadian way.

The Presbyterian Church did not have service on Christmas morning so we went to the Reformed Episcopal with my sister; Father stayed home with Mother.

All the week before Christmas we had been in and out of a sort of hole under the Reformed Church, sewing twigs of pine onto long strips of brown paper. These were to be put round the church windows, which were very high. It was cold under the church and badly lighted. We all sneezed and hunted round for old boards to put beneath our feet on the earth floor under the table where we sat pricking ourselves with holly, and getting stuck up with pine gum. The prickings made the ladies' words sharp—that and their sniffy colds and remembering all the work to be done at home. Everything unusual was fun for us children. We felt important helping to decorate the Church.

Present-giving was only done to members in one's immediate family. Others you gave love and a card to, and kissed the people you did not usually kiss.

From *The Book of Small*

Emily Carr, one of Canada's great painters, was born in 1871 in Victoria, B.C. The youngest-but-one of nine children, she had a traditional English upbringing in a loving family. Her unique works of the forests, Native villages and poles took her to remote parts of the West Coast.

Although she had always written, she turned to it full-time when her health began to fail. Her book *Klee Wyck*, about her home and pets, won a Governor General's Award. She also wrote *The Book of Small* and *The House of All Sorts*. She died in Victoria in 1945, where a small museum in her childhood home commemorates her life and art.

Clatsop County Plum Pudding

1 Plum Pudding Kettle (also known as a Steam Pudding Mold)
1/2 cup margarine
1 cup sugar
1 egg, unbeaten

Thoroughly mix by hand the ingredients below.

1 cup sifted flour	1 teaspoon nutmeg
1 teaspoon baking soda	1 cup fine dry bread crumbs
3/4 teaspoon cloves	1 cup chopped coarse walnuts
1 1/2 teaspoons cinnamon	1 1/2 cups raisins

In a large bowl with beater cream margarine, add sugar gradually, and beat in egg. Then add dry mixture with 3/4 cup hot water. Mixture should be stiff. Turn into well-greased pudding mold and snap on lid. Place kettle in preheated oven and cook for three hours at 250 degrees. Serves 8 people.

Serve hot with Hard Sauce or at room temperature with a lemon sauce.

Hard Sauce
1/2 teaspoon salt
1 egg white
1/4 cup brown sugar
1 egg yolk

Combine above in order until fluffy and fold in 1/2 cup heavy whipped cream.

This plum pudding is an annual fund-raiser for the Clatsop County Historical Society in Astoria, Oregon.

Friendly Overtures

by George H. Bird
Port Alberni, B.C., 1892

The first or second Christmas after I came here, some Indians came to our house in Alberni and asked us to go to the big communal house known as Old Tom's, on the Tse-shaht reserve. When my wife and I arrived, we found eight or nine other settlers had also been invited.

A Christmas tree was decorated in good style with ornaments. We were welcomed with friendly gestures and asked to be seated. I think the number of entertainers was seven: Gallic, Jaques and Fred were three of them. I have forgotten the others. They were all young men of about twenty years of age. They were dressed much alike, wearing white shirts. The downy feathers of wild geese or ducks had been sprinkled all over them. We were treated to a great

Interior of All Saints Church, Port Alberni, decorated for Christmas 1908 with evergreens and ferns.

show of vigorous dancing, to the accompaniment of singing, in which the other Indians present joined with much enthusiasm. They had composed a song in Chinook for our special benefit. It consisted of a welcome expressing friendly and well-disposed sentiments towards us who were now also dwellers in the fertile lands around about. While they sang, the drums were throbbing away. After an hour or so of entertainment, presents, consisting of baskets, mats and two or three little model canoes, were distributed amid considerable ceremony and applause.

At that time there had been little teaching of Christian ideals amongst the Indians here. They must have seen Christmas trees in some of the early settlers' homes, and the idea appealed to them. The Roman Catholic mission church had been established only a very few years. The Presbyterians had not started their school on the reserve. No Indian children had attended a regular school then. A few may have attended the Gill School, but that was newly established. Would it not have been more natural to think that we, with all our advantages of education and worldly possessions, ought to have been the hosts? After this friendly gesture, I always had a more kindly feeling towards the Indians and tried to make them realize it.

From *Tse-wees-tah—One Man in a Boat*

George Bird came to Vancouver Island from England in 1890. He and his wife had intended to visit Vancouver on their way to settle in Australia but they liked the West Coast so much they decided to stay. Bird had visited Australia in 1887 in charge of two railway locomotives that were to be exhibited in the Centennial Exhibition. In British Columbia, he worked for the Canadian Pacific Railway, and later as an engineer at Harrison Hot Springs. The couple also spent some time in Port Angeles, Washington and Nanaimo.

In 1892 they settled in Port Alberni, then called New Alberni. Bird was elected to city council when Port Alberni was incorporated in 1912. George Bird died in Port Alberni in 1954, when he was eighty-eight.

A Different Christmas Eve

by Reverend Alan Greene
Gerald Island, B.C., 1951

Different! How come? It's true that there isn't a great deal of difference between sheep and goats. And perhaps there hovered around the manger a few clucking fowl, who resented the disturbance of shepherds who for some strange reason visited the Bethlehem stable at midnight. Into this story of mine come goats, infuriated fowl, quacking ducks, a dog, a cat, and even goldfish. And instead of the Star of Bethlehem, a lighthouse with its alternating flashes, that pierced the dark waters of the Gulf of Georgia. A kindly mail carrier, a roaring tractor, a little life-boat, an eighteen-foot fisherman's skiff, a thirty-six-foot gas boat, an ex-cowpuncher, and a parson and two brave souls whose plans, if they were to share Christmas, called for immediate action on Christmas Eve . . . this amazing assortment of what we might call Props for the drama surely made this a story different from all other Christmas Eve stories. If the two kindly brave souls around whom the story wraps itself will forgive me, I will tell you just what happened.

I always try to visit the Ballenas Light Station and Gerald Island at Christmas, in the hope that if the weather allows of my lying at anchor off shore, I may give these island folks their Christmas Communion.

I left Lasqueti Island about four o'clock that Sunday afternoon, after a most heartening Christmas service in the new Church at False Bay. Fifty-three souls shared in the joy of Christmas-tide service. Darkness called for a compass course, and we hit Gerald Island dead on the nail. We went there first to see if Fred Bennett and his wife were both back in their little island home. Fred had been doing relief duty at the Ballenas Light Station and I thought he might be back home.

Dropping anchor two hundred feet off shore, I went ashore in the dinghy and found Mrs. Bennett all alone. Her husband was still at the lighthouse. They were both desperately anxious to know if his relief job might last long enough to warrant her joining him. A letter from the Light House Superintendent in Victoria would settle the problem. But this letter with all their Christmas mail was over on Vancouver Island. A maddening sequence of heavy storms had made it impossible for Fred to leave the lighthouse save for hurried trips between gales to Gerald Island, to see if his wife were all right. Gale warnings actually forbade his staying longer at his island home than to replenish the wood-pile, and then high-tail it back in his small 16-foot power-driven light-house tender to the Ballenas, where his first duty lay. That precious letter had actually reached the mail carrier's home half-way between Nanoose and Moorcroft, but there it lay amid a steadily accumulating mass of Christmas mail for the Bennetts. But it was more complicated than that. If the Department said O.K. to the move, what about all the stock on Gerald Island? It couldn't be left behind. And food supplies for both man and beast must be moved to the light-station. A simple plan presented itself to my mind. I'd go over to the Ballenas and pick Fred up early next morning and take him to Moorcroft, and he could go up the trail about two and a half miles to the mail carrier's, get the mail, and if the Chief in Victoria O.K.'d the move, we'd then go back to Gerald Island, and load all the gear and animals on the *John Antle*, and make a quick transfer to the Ballenas *if* the westerly holds off.

The relief to the distracted woman was indescribable. She had watched her husband make hazardous trips across the narrow three-mile stretch of stormy water in the little craft, till her courage was well nigh gone. He would disappear between great seas and finally she could only hope and pray he had made the lighthouse safely. It was hidden in behind a headland and she never saw its flashes at night. Days would pass without her knowing what his fate had been— till, to her immense relief, he came back home for an hour or two. If ever a soul prayed for her loved one's safety, she did, as she watched him in his little craft make the stormy crossing.

At 10 p.m. I went across to the Light Station in the *John Antle*, but I couldn't raise Fred in spite of many blasts on the ship's whistle. I think his radio

was on. So we ran in around the south end of the island and anchored, as we thought, for the night under the lea of a great kindly cliff. "Be ready, Frank, for a quick move if she changes to a south-easter." And she changed. At 2:30 a.m., a south-easter forced us to raise anchor and run for the shelter of Maggie Bay.

Three hours' sleep and then at seven-thirty we pulled out for the light-station and gave the keeper a mighty hail. "We're taking you to Moorcroft to get the mail, and then back to Gerald Island." "O.K." he shouted from the lighthouse. "I'll put the light out and join you at once." In ten minutes he was aboard and we headed for Vancouver Island. He made an amazingly fast trip out through the woods to the mail carrier's home. This good man stuffed about sixty pounds of mail in a huge haversack, and got the tractor in operation and at a roaring speed of about four miles an hour headed for the beach, only to be stopped by a big windfall. From there they packed the mail on their backs half-a-mile to the beach. "It's O.K. for us to make the move," said Fred. A few minutes and we were anchored off Gerald Island and went ashore to break the good news to madam. She had already packed a lot of gear, feeling it would work out this way. In no time she had served us a quick meal and then the fun began.

It was now Christmas Eve. And this is where the live-stock in this particular story comes in. They debated killing three of the goats and taking them "dressed" to the Ballenas. And killing off the fowl, fourteen hens. I saw delays that threatened the success of the whole plan as the weather reports promised a westerly that afternoon and that would absolutely rule out a landing with all this impedimenta.

Into the picture now comes my versatile side-kick, Frank Ball, whom I have correctly described as an ex-cowpuncher. Any man can pack sacks of grain, or spuds, or bales of hay. Or endless cartons of foodstuffs. Even my limited gifts were equal to this tedious business, and as quickly as madam filled a sack or a carton, it was under way down to the beach and out to the ship in our dinghy. I gave the two goldfish my most tender care as I packed them in a sealer out to the *John Antle*, plus a precious Christmas cactus that, full of a sense of fitness, had started to bloom and *must* be included in the cargo. Snow flurries and occasional westerly gusts urged us on. It had all the urgency of [Dunkirk]. Mrs. Bennett was very distressed at keeping us from reaching Vancouver that night, but I told her we were there till the job was done and they were settled on Ballenas. The Ballenas were to us what England was to the army trying to leave the shore of France. So, on with the job. We dragged a huge skiff down over logs, and it became the transport vessel for the live-stock and sundry bales of hay and a few sacks of chicken feed. Frank, with a boyhood background of Bible teaching a generation or two back in England, saw in me a Biblical figure whose name was Noah, of course, and the ark found its counterpart in the *John Antle*. As the problem of getting the stupid goats into crates and on board the skiff grew tougher and tougher, Frank's sympathy for Noah grew. Had our job been limited to two-of-a-kind like our famous forebear, it would have been simple. But there were five goats, fourteen hens, two bantams, four ducks, two goldfish, a dog and a cat to be moved. The goldfish and the bantams fitted the Biblical picture numerically, but the rest threw the whole thing out of focus.

Mrs. Bennett, with her great love for her animals, was all for gentle treatment. They had a crate ready for the birds, for each species, and a big crate for at least two of the goats. Here's where the cow-puncher touch came in. The two men entered the goat-shed, and fashioned halters, and brought the goats out one by one. The cold glittering eye of the old cow-puncher and his steady hand on the line around the nose of each beast (a patent hold Frank had used on bucking steers away back in Alberta), broke the spirit of the goats and after a few mad circles around Frank and his steady hold on the line, they recognized their master and apart from a few heaves over logs and a battle against boarding the skiff, they gave in, and in no time three huge goats were compressed into the crate. I was standing in the bow of the craft and heaving mightily from up forward. They had a far different expression than their forebears who entered the ark and gazed respectfully upon the patriarch who bade them come aboard. They fairly spat at me and with Frank's strangle-hold on their snouts, frothed at the mouth. They couldn't even bleat a curse upon me. Two year-old goats came next. The old cattle man neatly flipped them on to their backs and hog-tied them before the young things knew what had happened. Then while we kept madam busy locking up the house, we manhandled them into the bottom of the craft and there they lay.

By this time, Frank had a steely glint in his eye. He felt right at home. "Now for those birds." He waved aside the crates and said—"Sacks." The two men entered the chicken roost, and madam leaned against the door lest any of them fly out. I watched from across the pond. Inside, the uproar was awful as the men made wild passes at a cloud of birds that swept round and round them.

Once more Frank did his stuff. Fred made wild grabs at birds, missed them; but with a hand that got its bird every time, Frank reached out into the darkness of the little hut and snaffled a bird on the wing, and dropped it into a sack. Mrs. Bennett leaned against the door and covered her ears and almost wept for the poor birds. In no time, the men crossed the pond on a narrow plank causeway, each bearing about three bags of birds, including two sacks with quacking ducks, who seemed to take things much more calmly. The two bantams were tucked into a small shopping bag with a zipper. About an inch of zipper opening allowed of ventilation for the little fellows. They never uttered a cluck. The goldfish stared at me. Perhaps they were asleep. The dog and the cat took the whole episode as though trans-Pacific voyages were everyday experiences. As we towed the big skiff out to the *John Antle*, I, at first, sat in lordly style on top of the bales of hay, but Frank, who was doing all the real hard work, ordered me out of the craft and bade me ride in the dinghy. I obeyed. But once the sea-voyage to the Ballenas started, I took command as was fit and proper. I was back in my element and issued orders with quite a Nelson touch.

The Columbia *calls at one of the many floating logging camps along her coastal patrol.*

Landing the cargo was much simpler. The goats followed one another ashore in the style of the Pilgrim Fathers, so glad were they to escape from the confines of cribs and hog-tieings, but as soon as their hoofs touched terra firma they were off over the cliffs, and poor Fred went after them to get them into an old barn for shelter. They just laughed at him and he only succeeded in getting one old Nannie under cover.

I was watching the wind and the falling tide, and urged all the speed possible. After many comings and goings of the smaller craft everything was landed on the rocky shore and placed under cover for the night. I recalled a famous occasion when on the same shore I had landed a bride and groom in the persons of Mr. and Mrs. Alex Alliott one dark night after they were wedded aboard the *Columbia*. The groom, an old salt, ordered his bride to leap onto his back out of my dinghy, and she made a daring leap and they struggled ashore in the surf, under the kindly light of the *Columbia's* searchlight.

And so this Christmas Eve story ends. You ask, "What about the Christmas Communion?" I felt that our friends were so utterly weary and still had a lot of packing to do from the shore up to the lighthouse, and I suggested that we come back soon and give them their Christmas Communion when they were settled and rested in mind and body. I feel that there was something Sacramental in the service we had rendered them. I think the good Lord will feel that in bringing these two souls together for their Christmas Eve and Christmas Day, we had done something the Master would have commended. So we let it go at that.

In the gathering darkness, we headed south-east by east and made a perfect offing of Cape Roger Curtiss, and then picked up the flash of another Light, Point Atkinson, and from there headed in for Prospect Point and Coal Harbour.

We threw our lines onto the *Columbia* exactly at 9 p.m., where she lay at the Black Ball Towing Company Pier, and the Nine O'Clock Gun saluted us.

It was Christmas Eve.

From *The Log of the Columbia*, December 1951.

This story is from the New Series of *The Log of the Columbia*, an Anglican church magazine which began publishing in the 1930s and ceased in 1967. The mandate of the magazine was not to be a "mere record of passing events" but to "stand for the social, moral, and religious interests of the people of the district."

Metlakatla Christmas

by William Duncan
Annette Island, Alaska, 1888

The mail steamer *Idaho*, which we have been expecting for the last twelve days, arrived this morning, bringing us some freight from Portland. As our supply of flour and groceries was almost exhausted, and Christmas was very near,—the arrival of the steamer caused great rejoicing in the village, and especially among the children. Her delay, we were sorry to learn, was due to some crippling injuries she had sustained in a gale of wind on her last downward trip.

Sunday, December 23, 1888

Our unusually large attendance at church during the winter season was augmented to-day by the addition of some sixty or seventy strangers, who arrived here yesterday to spend Christmas with us. Though they came without being invited, they were heartily welcomed, and hospitably received, by our people. Our guests are from four native villages, and of two distinct languages;—both being very different to the language of the Metlakatlans.

Monday, January 7, 1889

Christmas and New Year is always a joyous season with the people of Metlakatla, and the last one has proved to be no exception to the rule. Though still living in temporary shanties, built among stumps and huge trees, both standing and fallen, yet the people are healthy and happy.

Fort Simpson, where the first Metlakatla village was located.

Some few days before Christmas the usual avocations of the natives are suspended,—smiling faces greet you everywhere, and the village storekeepers are overwhelmed with business.

The church elders hold meetings for the purpose of restoring the fallen, and reconciling to each other persons who have quarrelled.

On Christmas Eve there is a noticeable stillness outside, but the houses are illuminated. The waits are rehearsing their Christmas carols in the schoolroom, and I have deputations from the officials of the village,—council, elders, constables,—brass band, and fire brigade, to interrogate me about the proceedings of to-morrow. Late at night, the two men,—one being a born artist,—who have designed and secretly prepared some Christmas decorations, are busy arranging them in our temporary church. During the first hours of Christmas morning the voices of thirty of our young men are heard outside, singing hymns of praise, some in their own tongue, and some in English.

On Christmas morning, at 11 o'clock, our Church was crowded for divine service. The decorations were admirable, both in design and execution. The principle figure was an angel with outstretched wings, holding in each hand an olive branch, and supporting most gracefully, by both hands, a flying scroll, some thirty feet long, on which was written "On earth peace, good will to men. Nations shall learn war no more."

The service was commenced by chanting our Christmas song in Tsimshean; and, preceding the address, the choir sang the anthem, "God is the refuge of His people." The collection amounted to $130.08, the largest sum ever contributed by our people on one occasion. The money will be passed to the building fund for the proposed new church.

The afternoon was occupied with the children,—happy family indeed! 190 of whom received toys—while but five were sent empty away for misconduct.

From *The Apostle of Alaska* by John W. Arctander

British-born William Duncan was only twenty-five years old when, in 1857, he landed at Fort Simpson, an isolated Hudson's Bay Company fort on the northwest coast of B.C. Metlakatla was outside the walls of the fort, about twenty-five miles north of the present Prince Rupert.

Duncan devoted the rest of his life to introduce the Native people to Christianity. By 1874, he had transformed the village into a showplace. The church was the largest north of San Francisco, holding twelve hundred people. Duncan, however, became embroiled in a power struggle with the church leaders, who did not share his understanding of the Native people. Duncan was also battling the province, and Ottawa, over Native land claims, as he wanted the people to have more control over their land. Eventually, a bitter Duncan moved his Tsimshean flock to Alaska, to build a new community in the wilderness on Annette Island sixty miles to the northwest. New Metlakatla flourished. Duncan died in 1918 and is buried near his new church.

The *Southerner* Comes to Grief

by James A. Gibbs
Tillamook Head, Oregon, 1854

The first passenger steamer lost on the shores of Washington was the *Southerner,* a venerable 339-ton sidewheeler of the vintage of 1847. After three owners and three changes of name within slightly over two years she became a ship of little distinction. Her checkered career continued, and five years later after a complete rebuilding she was placed in Pacific coastwise service under the name *Southerner.*

After but two brief voyages she cleared San Francisco on December 20, 1854, in command of Captain F.A. Sampson, making calls at Eureka and Crescent City. She continued northward with but 25 paying passengers and a crew of 19. The ship's itinerary called for stops at Port Orford and Umpqua but at both places rough bar conditions prevented an entrance. The *Southerner* continued northward in a zigzag course like an inebriate after a night of celebration.

The winds continued kicking up from the southwest and the ocean became cantankerous. At 10 a.m. on Christmas Day, Oregon's Tillamook Head was reached but most of the passengers were confined to their cabins with bad cases of *mal de mer*. The Yuletide spirit was forgotten. Three hours later the vessel gained the Columbia River entrance but the winds had made the bar a mass of white fury. While the steamer wallowed about off the mouth of the river the chief engineer summoned the bridge with the news that the vessel had developed a serious leak below the waterline. The passengers were immediately alerted to the impending danger, but most were too sick to care.

Captain Sampson stood off the bar until 6 p.m. Then, conditions failing to improve, he set his course for Puget Sound. All the time water was gaining in the hold in spite of the full output of the pumps. When the situation reached alarming proportions the captain ordered every male passenger to join a bucket brigade. Even those who were green from seasickness were pressed into the

Greetings from the Union Steamship line-up.

task, gagging and moaning as they passed each container. The combined efforts of crew and passengers managed to keep the inrush of water at a level with the engine room floor.

At daybreak on December 26, the engines were barely turning over—the vessel laboring heavily. Fearing the worst, the shipmaster ordered the quartermaster to bring the steamer nearer the shore. Close-hauled to the wind, movement was at a snail's pace until late afternoon. In spite of the efforts to prevent it, water had now reached alarming heights and the stern had begun to drop. The passengers pleaded with the captain to beach the ship. Some even threatened him. But he didn't have to be threatened, for none knew better than he the danger and responsibility resting on him. He shouldered aside the tormenting words of the passengers and ordered his mate to keep a gun handy in case of necessity. When the steamer's forward progress was all but halted she came to anchor in seven fathoms southeast of Cape Flattery. Her position offered little protection and the seas pounded so relentlessly that she creaked in every joint. Mild panic broke out among the passengers and the mate's hand slipped into his pocket for his gun. But the officer's harsh words were sufficient to keep them under control. Such a severe punishment did the steamer take that at last it slipped its anchor chains and was carried broadside onto an inundated shoal amid screams of terrified souls.

The captain sprang into instant action. He ordered the masts cut and jettisoned. Then her stack was pried from its fittings and dropped overboard. The vessel, thus lightened of some of its burden, was carried over the reef and swept into the breakers. Her decks dipped into the sloshing surf and breaker after breaker swept her higher and higher. The wind was strong, the tide full, and the dying steamer—nearly on her beam ends—thumped over the reef, coming to rest among the driftwood. Frozen with fear, the men and women on the Southerner remained almost motionless until the tide ebbed and left the battered wreck in temporary repose. By morning, amazed at their survival, all hands evacuated their wooden prison. There was not one casualty. The *Southerner* had delivered its cargo of humans but the next rising sea, fortified by powerful breakers, pounded the old sidewheeler into submission and she caved in like a straw hut in a windstorm.

The survivors travelled on foot to Neah Bay, many weary miles without complaint. They had been resurrected from the cradle of the deep, and when men are saved from almost certain death they can smile where others would gnash their teeth. The *Southerner* reached the port of no return but her human cargo went free.

From *Shipwrecks of the Pacific Coast*

In the last century, hundreds of sailing ships and small steamers met their end on the rugged western edge of North America where it meets the Pacific. Shipwrecks are rarer now, but the turbulent seas and the ragged coast still claim ships and those who sail them.

A Surprise Package

by Harriet Fish Backus
Britannia Beach, B.C., 1910

Christmas was nearing and even on the quiet beach we felt the excitement that everywhere stirs emotions at that time of year.

As on our first Christmas at the Tomboy [mine], the Batchellers invited us to spend the day with them.

"Come early Christmas morning and bring your presents," said Beth. "We'll all open them together and it will be fun to watch Edgar and Harriet."

George and Jim cut two stately fir trees from the forest. Ours graced our dining room. With strings of popped corn and cranberries draped over the branches, the little ornamental angel from George's childhood over the top, candles in their holders, we were ready to light the tree—beautiful!

The day before Christmas Beth and I, with our babies, strolled to the wharf eagerly waiting for the mail bags. "Here she comes!" Our usual shout.

The sky was dark and the water gray. The *Britannia* was plowing a furrow through choppy seas. She reversed from the pier and repeatedly tried to dock against the haul and shoving of tide and wind. Finally the mail bags were tossed onto the pier, bulging as if Santa Claus had been most generous.

Seeing Beth, the freight clerk called to her, "Is Mr. Batcheller coming here today?"

"No," she answered. "He's at the mine."

"I have something for him," added the clerk.

"I'll take it," Beth offered. But the clerk hesitated, turning the package this way and that. "It's marked 'fragile' and 'personal' but I guess it's all right to leave it with you," he said handing it to her.

In his buggy Edgar was peeking from behind a mound of paper bags and boxes, groceries and goodies for Christmas. Beth moved them about to make room for Jim's package, and looking at the postmark said, "I can't imagine who could be sending us a present from Vancouver." She placed the package in the buggy and shook her head wondering. "I'd better not put it where Edgar can reach it. He might knock it off, and it could be china or glassware."

"Let me carry it," I said. "I'm going to the post office and then I'll bring it to you."

"All right. I want to get this turkey home. Poor Edgar, he's weighed down with all these packages." And off she went, pushing the loaded buggy over the tracks and across the bridge.

The package, bound round and round with strong cord, was not heavy but there was no place on Harriet's go-cart to hold it; the cart took both my hands to push it over the frozen, bumpy road. So I crooked my little finger tightly under the cord. A strong wind was blowing and swinging the package back and forth. The word FRAGILE in bold red letters prompted me to dig the weighted finger deeper into my palm.

At the store I placed it on the counter while Syd sorted the mail. Slipping ours into a paper bag, I squeezed it tightly behind Harriet, slid the cord of Jim's package again over my finger and walked briskly to Beth's—over the tracks and

A snowfall at Britannia Beach around the turn of the century entices the hardy to enjoy the outdoors. (Photographer Philip Timms.)

across the bridge which was now bouncing and swaying from side to side. The cord was cutting deeper into my finger so I pushed the go-cart faster.

Beth's tree was beautifully decorated with bright ornaments, packages tied in green or red paper, and ribbons tucked between the branches. Boxes, big and little, covered the floor around and beneath the green plumes of the stately fir.

"Where shall I put this package, Beth?" I asked.

"On the floor with the others," she said and went on draping the bookcase with scented branches of cedar. [. . .]

As I started for home, the tide was flooding in, water creeping up near Beth's porch. The rickety footbridge swayed violently and the wind blew me against the handrail. I hurried home to prepare for my husband's prodigious appetite and the three young men from the boardinghouse whom George had invited for the evening.

After dinner we lit the candles on the tree and enjoyed the company of our visitors.

On Christmas morning the ground was white with snow and a light covering draped the trees in gauzy whiteness, patterned with clusters of green showing through, and the wind had died down. A beautiful Christmas Day!

We ate a hearty breakfast, fed the chickens, gathered our packages and set out down the road for Beth's.

Everything seemed deserted except for our Japanese neighbor who was repairing his fence, for this was the only day of the year when the entire operations of the mine and mill stopped. The miners weren't digging, the tram wasn't running, the mill was silent, and no ore barges were loaded. The prevailing quiet was uncanny. There was peace in our world at Britannia Beach and I could say truly "Good will toward all men."

Perhaps, too, it was an uneasy peace. Silence around a mill is disturbing, creating the feeling of a ghost town.

The footbridge over the rocks was slippery. But "Merry Christmas," we shouted, entering the house so decked and festive in holiday finery.

We began opening gifts. One entire sack had come from Beth's relatives in Massachusetts. Harriet ran back and forth, often falling down in her excitement with Edgar creeping his fastest to keep up with her. Mittens, scarfs, books, toys, were unwrapped and the brightly colored trimmings tossed aside until we were in the middle of chaos.

"Jim, open that package from Vancouver," Beth urged. "I forgot to tell you about it when you came home last night, and I can hardly wait to know who sent it."

Jim cut the cord, took off the wrapping paper and lifted the lid of a box. I saw the startled look and the color drain from his face. He turned to Beth and sharply asked, "Who gave this to you?"

"The freight clerk on the *Britannia,*" she replied, surprised at his agitation.

"I have to go to the office, right now. I'll be back soon."

With no explanation Jim pulled on his coat and hat and hurried out with the box, leaving us utterly bewildered.

The remaining gifts were left unopened while we played with the children and waited, perplexed and curious, for Jim's return. We had not long to wait.

Beth met him at the door. "Jim, what in the world is the matter? Wasn't that a present for you?"

"*That* package," he said gravely, "contained four thousand standard blasting caps. If it had been dropped, none of us would be here now."

Exclamations sputtered from Beth and me. George looked at Jim as if he couldn't believe what he had heard and as if it couldn't have happened. Beth had handled the package of death. Edgar's plump hands had slapped it. I had swung it from my finger against the handle of the go-cart. I recalled how it had touched the bridge railing more than once as the wind blew me against it. I had placed it none too gently on the store counter and under the Christmas tree.

Such things as these caps were *never* handled except by those in authority. No explosives of any kind were allowed aboard the *Britannia,* a freighter—but also a passenger vessel!

The mine, having run short of caps, had sent to Vancouver for an emergency order to be shipped up on the next ore scow. But it had just left when the order was received. It would be a week before the next trip. Contrary to all rules and regulations, and unknown to Jim, the caps had been shipped on the *Britannia*, addressed to him, the superintendent.

Our Christmas joy was considerably quieter and we were most thankful for the gift of gifts to us all, and many more in Britannia Beach . . . life itself.

From *Tomboy Bride*

Britannia, the copper mine on the east shore of Howe Sound for which the town of Britannia Beach is named, began operating at the turn of the century. In its heyday, the 1920s, it was the largest copper mine in the British Empire. The mine closed in 1974 after an eventful life during which it produced 52 million tons of ore and employed 60,000 people. Although close to Vancouver, access was by sea only for much of the mine's life. The mine site is now the British Columbia Museum of Mining, complete with underground tours.

George Backus was a mining graduate from the University of California School of Mines. The Backus family were at Britannia Beach from 1910 to 1912.

A Snowy Wedding

by Dr. John Helmcken
Victoria, B.C., 1852

The day before the time fixed it snowed and it snowed—lord, how it snowed!—so that a couple of feet of snow lay on the ground. The only thing approaching to a carriage was a two-wheeled light cart—the governor's carriage—useless, there not being any roads. The bridegroom (himself) goes to church. The bride (his intended) and her maidens at home, waiting for the carriage. The cart was at the fort, had travelled a hundred yards, the wheels no longer would turn and there was a dead stop. The charioteer, a lively, active, good-natured French-Canadian gentleman, full of resource, got an idea. He sent to the store for a dry-goods box, cut off the top and one side, put a seat in and threw some scarlet cloth over all. Having hewn a couple of willows growing close at hand, of these he made shaft and runners all in one! The box arriving is fixed upon the willow runners, the horse harnessed, the sleigh hastens for the bride and maids.

An early, flowery Christmas card.

The poor bridegroom is waiting impatiently in the mess-room church; the hour approaches twelve! His best man rushes into the mess-room, to put the clock hands back, when he suddenly encounters the chaplain's wife, dismayed he kicks out a dog, to disguise his intentions, and returns disappointed. The chaplain appears, and says, if the bride does not arrive before twelve, it only wants a quarter now, I will not be able to perform the ceremony today, it being illegal to do so. Here's a pretty kettle of fish; but just then the tinkle of the sleigh bells are heard, and the bridesmaids and dry-goods box appear. The whole party hurry into the church, the ceremony is proceeding, the clock strikes twelve, just as the ring is put on the finger, etc.: the ceremony over, the bride and bridegroom leave the church to return to their parents' house for a good time, and then the guns roar from the bastions. The bell in the middle of the fort rings—the dogs howl thereunder—the men fire muskets—all hurrah. Grog is served out all round, there is feasting, revelling and jollity, and everybody heart and soul wishes the handsome, favorite and favored couple very many happy new years. . . .

From *The Reminiscences of John Sebastian Helmcken*

This amusing description of his simple Christmas wedding to Cecilia Douglas (the daughter of Governor James Douglas) was by John Sebastian Helmcken. Later, as Victoria grew, society weddings became elaborate and served to indicate a family's social position.

Dark Christmas Cake

1 cup dark raisins

1 cup sultana raisins

3/4 cup currants

2/3 cup mixed candied fruit

2/3 cup red and green cherries

2/3 cup mixed peel

1 cup blanched slivered almonds

1 1/4 cups all-purpose flour, sifted

1/2 teaspoon baking powder

1/4 teaspoon baking soda

1/4 teaspoon salt

1/4 teaspoon mace

1 teaspoon cinnamon

1/2 cup butter

3/4 cup brown sugar

3 large eggs

2 tablespoons currant jelly

If desired, 1/4 cup of rum, brandy or sherry can be sprinkled over fruit and nuts and left overnight. Cover. Stir once or twice.

Preheat oven to 275 degrees. Line two loaf pans with two layers of waxed paper each. Sift flour and measure, set aside. Measure fruit and nuts into a large bowl, sprinkle with 3/4 cup of measured flour and stir well to coat and separate fruit, set aside. Sift remaining flour with baking powder, baking soda, salt, mace and cinnamon into a bowl, set aside. In a large bowl, cream butter and gradually add brown sugar. Add eggs one at a time to creamed mixture, beating well with each addition. Add dry ingredients to creamed mixture and beat thoroughly, then beat in currant jelly. Using a wooden spoon, stir in floured fruit and nut mixture, stirring until all fruit is coated with batter. Divide batter evenly between pans, packing well into corners and spreading evenly. Make a shallow trench down centre of loaf.

Place a shallow pan of water in oven to keep cake moist, and bake for two to three hours until done.

Cool slightly before removing from pans, and let cool thoroughly on rack. Wrap in foil and store in airtight container in cool place. Sprinkle with a few tablespoons of brandy, rum or sherry occasionally.

About a week before Christmas, cover with almond paste and butter icing, or just icing. Store in container with tight-fitting lid.

Rich Butter Icing
1/4 cup unsalted butter
3 tablespoons whipping cream
2 cups sifted icing sugar
1/2 teaspoon almond or vanilla extract

Cream butter, and add about 2 tablespoons of icing sugar. Add extract and blend well. Gradually add whipping cream. Add enough icing sugar to make a thick icing, adding more sugar or cream as necessary. Spread over top and sides of cake.

Tobogganing and Christmas still go together.

A Foggy Christmas Eve

by L.H. Roberts
Roberts Creek, B.C., early 1900s

As Christmas had, as it were, sneaked up on us unawares, we were a bit late sending in our food order and, though we thought it should have been down there in time, the last steamer before Christmas came up and there was nothing on it for us. While we would not really be short of food it would be far from what we expected for this festive season.

I was making up the mail bag ready for the down boat. Ida had said again about not having a single orange or any Christmas food. I glanced over my shoulder and said, "Christmas hasn't come yet and when it does it may bring us lots of things."

"If Christmas never came again you would just go along as you do. But, thank goodness, everyone isn't like you!" she snapped in her frustration. This hurt me a bit. Then I realized, to some extent, it was true. Mother had always made Christmas a good time in England and last year we were with Dan's big, happy family but now we were established and on our own we must make our own good time. I hadn't given it a thought. But what could we do? Oh, well, something would come to me.

I had given the horses their dinner and was going to the house when the steamer yelled of her approach. I ran and grabbed the mail bag and went to the beach, pulled the boat off the drift log and was beside the steamer when an idea hit me and I called to the mate, "Pull her up, John. I'm going with you." [. . .]

The Skipper said, "Does your Old Man know you're aboard?"

"If he were looking he probably does by now. None of them knew any more than I did till I was alongside."

"I felt damned sure about that when I saw your boat coming aboard. What's the matter, Harry, if I'm not butting in too much?"

"Not a darned thing came up, so we're stranded for Christmas."

"Got any money with you?"

I had not thought about that and I said with sudden dismay, "Gee! Not a cent! Guess there wasn't much more ashore, either."

"How much would carry you over? How are you going back?" he asked.

"I guess ten dollars. I'm rowing back up as soon as I get a few odd bits."

"Take the wheel. I'll go round up a ten spot." I was alone for a few minutes. What would I get to take back; a big turkey and—the wheelhouse door opened and the skipper came in.

"Here you are—twenty in small bills—and if you need more I was to tell you some of them will be aboard all night; just let them know." I was almost overwhelmed at their kindness, and to hide my feelings I stuffed the money in my pocket, thanked him briefly and began talking of something else.

We ran into fog at the east end of Bowen Island and it became thicker as we neared the city. For the first time I felt a bit worried. This was Christmas Eve. How would I get back in time? If it got very thick perhaps I couldn't travel at all. I had no compass. It wasn't too bad yet. Perhaps if I hurried—

We passed no other boat and made a landing without too much trouble. I was the first ashore and was lost before getting clear of the railway tracks. Then I ran into the Skipper who steered me to Water St. We turned and went west. "I'll go along and let my brother know who you are. He has a wholesale store—poultry, fruit and vegetables—and you can get most of what you want from him."

I soon had things collected and was asking about candy. "Sorry, we don't have any. But wait. I'll soon have some over from across the street." I protested but he was phoning and I heard him say, "Make this in one minute or it's too late."

When I asked what I owed, I was astonished to hear him say, "Oh, this is on my big brother. He'll fix this up. It's all right. You get on your way. I'll go with you to the corner."

I assured him that wasn't necessary as I had counted my steps—"two hundred and twenty to the corner then fifty, then ninety and I'm there." He laughed. We exchanged good wishes and I was off and got to the steamer without mishap.

Aboard I found John, the mate, with a few of the crew and friends around the big table and the smell of hot food made me realize how hungry I was, so I sat down and after a fine meal and all their good wishes for luck on the trip home I got into my boat and was off. The last I heard was John saying, "Why, Hell! You couldn't lose Harry out there. Fog, snow or what have you he'll be there at the Christmas dinner tomorrow or hell will freeze over!"

Visit the bright lights—Union Steamships poster advertising Christmas in Vancouver.

I wished I could feel as confident as John. I didn't like leaving for the twenty-five-mile trip in that fog. It was like midnight though that was many hours off yet. The fog made it penetratingly cold after the warmth of the salon and I pulled up my coat collar and shrank into it.

The sound of the bell at Brockton Point was coming over clear; no sound of another boat but I must remember the Howe Sound steamer would be coming. [. . .]

I stood and pushed the oars before me; made the point and headed out of the Narrows helped by a strong tide. I stayed with this run as I had the Narrows to myself, as far as I could hear.

When I got to the outer corner, or Prospect Point, I could hear the short toots of the Sound steamer trying to tell the skipper where he was by the echo. He was not, I knew, where he expected, so I pushed my boat towards him hoping I could do something. I went as close as I dared then yelled, "You're almost over to Siwash Rock, Jack."

"Who in hell is telling me," came down from over my head.

"It's me. I'm on my way home to the Creek, Jack. I've just come out of the Narrows. You're nearly over to the rock and closer in than you think. I'd back up a little."

"Oh, I got you now. Thanks a lot, Harry. I'd hate to be on *your* trip tonight. All the best and Merry Christmas!"

[. . .] The three short blasts rolled off the high bluff. Then I waited till he gave the single longer blast indicating he was moving ahead. Now I pushed on toward the lighthouse over to starboard [Point Atkinson] the horn of which I could hear but the light was not visible for it was five miles away. By its intermittent blasts I kept my bow well over to the shore as the running out tide would pull me to the Point Grey side.

It seemed a long way and when I got there I was fairly tired. [. . .] I stopped under the beam of the light for a moment. Now came a stretch of wide open water. Would I risk crossing or not? Then, I dug my oars deep with my whole weight behind them and was away for the corner of Bowen Island.

As the crow flies, this would be about three miles but would I go as the crow? There happened to be a large boat over near Point Grey with the bell telling me she was not moving. With this and the fog horn at Atkinson I was able to hold a course to the point of Bowen Island. It was rather like holding on to two lines, affixed to these places, which played out as you went. One you knew must come at an angle, the other from straight behind, and though I don't remember thinking of it at the time it was like so many incidents that have occurred in my life—when my need was great the help was always there.

Rowing is conducive to thinking and my mind was covering a wide range when suddenly I was jerked back to the foggy waste of water I was traversing by a horn, muted but right ahead—I was standing at the time. Now what, I asked myself. Yes, there it was again. I turned about. Listened. Then I heard Atkinson's horn far ahead and over my shoulder came the echo right off the point of Bowen Island so around I went again, and straight ahead for another hundred miles, or was it one? I was really very tired by the time I saw the point.

The fog was not as thick and I could dimly see the shoreline. Soon I was passing the bay where a house was. I saw a light at the beach. Yes, I would row in there. I heard a voice say, "I hear someone rowing. Yes, I see a rowboat."

"No one else but Santy himself would be coming in here at this time." Laughter and two forms moved right in front at the water's edge. The light was held up and two faces looked at me.

"Is it you, Roberts, of Robert's Creek? Yes, yes, it is and you are just the one we need right now. Where in Heck have you been? Are you lost? Come on, we'll pull the boat out. Tide is falling."

I had met the young fellow before. Ted had sailed up coast to Sechelt and, on his way back, had been caught by a bad sou'easter; too much for his boat so had stayed with us at the Creek. He and his sister, Nat, were down at the shore now.

They were having a Christmas Eve party which included many small children; also there was a "big" little, eight-year-old, city slicker who didn't believe in Santa and was disappointing the other children with his cynicism.

I was tired and hungry and playing Santa was the last thing I wanted but all had gone so well for me I felt I ought to. I don't think I reasoned this out. It was probably a sort of conditioned reaction as Granny and Mother had dinned into me that one of the Natural Laws of life was *sharing*—a natural give and take. I had taken a lot of kindness this night. Now it was time to give.

In a few minutes I'd forgotten my tiredness and was entering into the fun as they dressed me up in Dad's old red dressing gown (which had to be pinned up over a foot, for Dad was tall) and big rubber boots. With a big hat and white fluffy scarf there was little but my face showing.

With all my new accoutrements it was no easy job getting to the house alone in the dark. The other two had been gone some time. I peeped in at the window and watched the people as they sat around the big room, lit by lamps, a big open fire and the sparkle of the Christmas tree tinsel and ornaments. I turned the front door handle and made an imposing entrance by tripping and, to a chorus of exclamations, I sprawled suddenly among them. I got clear of the door, kicked it shut and said, "Oh, Oh, by

Cover of Birks' 1924 Christmas yearbook.

Gosh! What a night! Was on my way to Sechelt and almost missed your light in the fog but here I am safe and sound."

The two smallest children ran yelling to the kitchen and the others, young and old, gathered round as I seated myself on the floor. Then I noticed the little city slicker, smartly dressed, not far from me so I grabbed him and pretended I was going to spank him then turned his face to me and lectured him about letting me down.

By that time Nat had brought me a hot drink and the two smallest dared venture near and stood wide-eyed, gazing. But what I enjoyed most was the mystification of the adults. You could see them counting noses and saying: Everyone is here. Who in the world is this?

Then I mentioned I'd left my sack outside so Nat and Ted brought in a bulging bag of gifts and soon there were bright ribbons and tissue paper all over the floor; the delightful din of excited children yelling and laughing; the merry music of whistles, horns and squeaks of new toys and such a hub-bub you could hardly hear yourself think.

But mothers soon decided it was time for little ones to be in bed and off they went happily hugging their gifts and chattering excitedly. I was very glad for with the warmth of the room and all my new trappings I was about bursting with heat.

We older ones gathered round the freshly-made-up fire for coffee and sandwiches and a good talk. My identity was known now and there was an old navy man among the crowd who marvelled at my rowing from Vancouver on such a night. This man had never been around the Horn and when he heard my father had been more than once he said, "Now, you've let the cat out of the bag. You're just a very big chunk off the old block!" Our tongues were all loosened and several hours slipped by as we yarned. Finally we said goodnight and parted.

The house became quiet. It had been arranged that I would be called after three hours sleep. Ted and Nat would have breakfast ready. I was by the open fire under the big dressing robe.

I seemed to have only just fallen asleep and had to drag myself up from the depths of the earth when I felt a hand laid on my shoulder. We had a good breakfast and were off down to my boat. Nat and Ted decided to come with me while I was going down the face of the island.

There was a little wind as we pushed off so I stepped the mast and hoisted sail. When we got clear of the bay and the sail filled, the three of us settled like three young birds in the nest with the girl jammed tight between us two boys for it was cold in the early morning air. As we sailed the wind gathered force as if to hurry us to our destination.

"I don't think I should try to land you at the point. Is there any corner where you could get ashore better?" I asked.

"Yes, I think we could make it all right at the next corner." At this Nat started unbuttoning the row of big buttons which ran down the front of her navy skirt.

I looked at her puzzled, and said, "Now, don't get ready to swim ashore. The sea isn't that bad."

She just looked at me and went back to the buttons. Then came, "Now, Mister, I'm able to jump as far as you. You may look. See for yourself." The fairly long skirt (of that day) had turned into a pair of long pants (my first view of a divided skirt) and I watched two boys as they jumped ashore. They climbed to a higher point and stood watching me as the wind and sea gathered strength. But with the weight of the two removed, the stern was lighter so I was ready to take it.

By the time I had gotten to Gower Point the sail was acting more as a big flag before the mast. With tide, wind and sea I was racing homeward, and dared not gather too much wind. The big white horses seemed to always catch me up and before I came to the bay where our house stood I was asking myself if I should have to pass it and run on to shelter around Mission Point.

The tide was low enough that great white combers were rolling over the flat sand and breaking just over the edge of the gravel beach, where I saw the whole family standing ready should I try to land. My homing instinct was strong and just at this moment I caught sight of an extra big, crested wave rolling towards me so swung the sail to port and was picked up and rushed shoreward atop of it, like riding a surf board. I remember feeling the boat jar sharply as it dropped hard on the gravel where it was grabbed by all hands, including my own, for I leapt out the second I felt it land. We carried it up and over the drift logs where it would be safe from the sea and these logs which often jumped and rolled at high tide (making an intermittent roll of thunder with each new wave) with such a wind as this.

When we were in and I was recounting my adventures, Ida squealed with delight as she pulled a big turkey from the sack and ran to me with a hug and,

"Harry, I'm sorry I said what I did. Forget it please. Now do go and get some sleep and I'll waken you in time for Christmas dinner." And that's exactly what I did.

After Christmas and when we were expecting the first steamer with mail I had gotten help to get the boat back over the logs and down to the water, which was very calm. We pushed the boat in and, to our amazement, we watched water coming through the bottom seams as if it were a basket. We left it there and I ran after the other small boat which was at the creek shelter.

I had two ten dollar bills which I offered to the Skipper to replace the money which he had loaned me and thank him for the goods.

"No, no," he protested, "I was telling the manager of the Company (The Union Steamship Company) about your trip and he said this would be on them for a Christmas box to you so he fixed it with me." They were all so interested in how I got home in the fog that the boat was held while I told my story and none, not even the passengers, seemed to mind the delay.

But that was the old rowboat's swan song. The jar of landing on the gravel had loosened every seam and it was beyond repair. It had made a "special" trip and it could never be used again just as a wine glass was broken after a very special toast.

From *The Trail of Chack Chack*

Harry Roberts was sixteen when he and his family came to British Columbia from England in 1898. The family settled on the Sunshine Coast at what became known as Roberts Creek. Fascinated by the sea, he served as cook, mate, engineer or skipper on many boats and explored the coast sometimes by design, other times by accident. His adventures made him well known all along the coast. Eventually, Harry settled at Billings Bay on Nelson Island.

Far from Home

by Reverend John Sheepshanks
New Westminster, B.C., 1859

On Christmas Eve (1859) I spent the day in calling upon all those who, as far as I could judge, ought to be impelled to keep the birthday of the dear Lord in such a way as would be acceptable to Him, by coming to our worship to offer their spiritual sacrifices of praise and thanksgiving and to partake of the Blessed Sacrament. But I found very little encouragement.

It was a miserable evening; a soft mild wind was blowing, drizzle was falling; it was soon pitch dark, and in the neighbourhood of the huts and stores the mud was deep and sticky. I floundered about in the darkness, occasionally tripping over a stump, feeling very warm in the moist air with my waterproof garments; and now and then, when down by the riverside, I heard the voices of men in the drinking-bars shouting and singing, and the light gleaming from the saloon fell upon the black mud and cast-away playing cards that I was treading underfoot. And I thought of happy scenes at home, and old friends at Leeds, and the dignified, uplifting services at the parish church.

Reverend Sheepshanks poses for the camera; inset, as Bishop of Norwich.

But still, it was all right. It was delightful having the society of friendly, highly educated men at the camp. We had a nice number of communicants on Christmas morning, and the message of Christmas is always one of "good news."

From *A Bishop in the Rough*

The Reverend John Sheepshanks, later Bishop of Norwich, came to Canada in 1859 from Leeds, England. He was rector of Holy Trinity Church, New Westminster. A man with a wry sense of humor—and, according to Dr. John Helmcken, a prodigious appetite—Sheepshanks was an enthusiastic traveller. He explored North America, Mexico and Jamaica. In 1867, he returned to England the long way around, visiting Hawaii, China, Asia and Russia, including Siberia. He arrived in England in November 1867, and became Bishop of Norwich in 1908. Of his journal, he says, "I had always, even in trying circumstances, at the gold-mines of Cariboo or on the arid steppes of Asia, kept a fairly full journal."

(Incidentally, Reverend Sheepshanks bought a parcel of virtual wilderness near Burrard Inlet shortly before he left Canada. He paid a small sum each month on the property and gave the deed to the church, asking the Bishop to continue the payments. In 1894, in England, he asked the Bishop, "'Well, my dear Bishop, and what became of the piece of land which I gave you for the Church on Burrard's Inlet?' The good man positively blushed as he said, 'If I had kept that piece of land, it would have sufficed to endow the whole diocese.' It occupied the very centre of Vancouver.")

Eating Crow

by James G. Swan
Shoal-Water Bay, Washington, 1852

As Christmas drew near the game seemed to decrease; and, although we had a plenty of salt salmon and potatoes, we thought we could not celebrate the day without having a goose, or duck, or some kind of bird; but nothing came near us but crows. The captain said crow was good, so was eagle, so was owl; he reasoned in this manner: A crow, said he, is good, because it has a crop like a hen; and eagles, hawks, and owls are good, for, although they have no crops, yet they do not feed upon carrion. So we addressed ourselves to the subject of procuring a Christmas dinner. Fortunately or unfortunately, I shot a couple of crows. They were very ancient, entirely void of fat, and altogether presented to my mind a sorry picture of a feast. But the captain was delighted. "I will make a sea-pie of them," said he, "and then you can judge what crow-meat is." The birds were cleaned and cut up, and a fine sea-pie made with dumplings, salt pork, potatoes and a couple of onions. And precisely at meridian on Christmas-

A tough old bird.

42

day (for the old captain liked to keep up sea-hours), the contents of the iron pot were emptied into a tin pan, and set before us smoking hot.

I tried my best to eat crow, but it was too tough for me. "How do you like it?" said the old man, as, with a desperate effort, he wrenched off a mouthful from a leg. "I am like the man," said I, "who was once placed in the same position: 'I ken eat crow, but hang me if I *hanker* arter it'." "Well," says the captain, "it *is* somewhat hard; but try some of the soup and dumplings, and don't condemn crow-meat from this trial, for you shot the grandfather and grandmother of the flock: no wonder they are tough; shoot a young one next time." "No more crow-meat for me, thank you," said I. So I finished my Christmas dinner on dumpling and potatoes.

From *The Northwest Coast; or, Three Years Residence in Washington Territory*

James Gilchrist Swan did what many people dream of doing. Aged thirty-four, a very proper New Englander, he left his family and prosperous ship-fitting business in Boston to take part in the California Gold Rush. After barely three months in California, Swan sailed to Vancouver Island, where he had decided to live. He found the British unfriendly, and soon returned to San Francisco. There he met Charles Russell, who lived in Shoalwater Bay. At Russell's urging, Swan left California for the Pacific Northwest to begin his adventures along the coast. He later settled in Port Townsend and became an Indian Agent at Neah Bay. He died around the turn of the century.

Christmas Crabs

by Sam L. Simpson
Ketchikan, Alaska, 1932

I suppose that this whole Ketchikan business could be called an adventure. Adventures, when you dissect them, are usually chronicles of hazards and hardships, much easier to enjoy in armchair reading than in the reality. This Ketchikan enterprise had all the earmarks of high adventure, dangers abounding, discomforts at times that bordered on pure misery, and the bait that led us on; some cash income that might be had out of it, a rare find in that winter of 1932–33. Looking back, it even had its moments of comedy. . . .

[Sam Simpson's family had a half share in an old boat, the *Ogden*—of which it was said "she rolls two days before a storm and three days after." Desperate for money, Simpson and his friend, Fred Windberg, had entered into a deal with two others to catch crabs in Naden Harbour, cook them in Ketchikan and ship them to Seattle.]

We returned to Prince Rupert to get a small boat powered with an old car engine that was Fred's only asset. We figured that we could use the small boat for fishing the crabs. After clearing customs we left Rupert with Fred's boat in tow. All went well until we passed Triple Island and started across the Straits. A nasty southwest wind came up right on our bow. The *Ogden* began to plunge into the oncoming waves and Fred's boat was dancing madly on its leash. If this kept up it was sure to either break our towline or spring a plank and sink. There was nothing for us but to go back.

At this point Fred suggested that we take shelter in Squaderee. You won't find Squaderee on the chart but you will find Qlawdzeet Anchorage, which is the same place, at the north end of Stephens Island. I had never been in this small harbour, which is a kind of jumping-off place for boats getting ready to cross to the Islands. Fred said that there was no problem, he had been in there more than once as a crew member on a halibut boat. What I did not take into account was that Fred had always been an engineer and had never paid attention to the sometimes tricky business of getting into one of these small harbours. That was always left to the skipper.

It was dark when we reached Squaderee. One of the winter snow squalls that a southwest gale sends along at that time of year came up just as we were trying for the entrance. Fred was out on the bow, piloting us in. The black land was suspiciously close, getting closer, so much so that I saw some trees reflected in the light from our open cabin door. Something was wrong! I was just reaching for the reverse when the Ogden's keel nudged the bottom and she came quietly to rest, stuck hard and fast. We backed up but to no avail. Then came the sickening realization. Looking at the tide book we saw that we had grounded right at the peak of the highest tide in December, and there would not be another one as high until early January.

The tide went out and the *Ogden* lay down on her side like some big beast that refuses to go any farther for her master. We had gone into a false entrance, right over a horrifying collection of reefs and rocks, and so far up on the beach that the top of our leaning mast was almost touching the trees alongside. We were perfectly safe, no surf came in this far. But how to get out? We had no radio of course, no fish boats did then, and at that time of the year no boats could be expected to come around. It was the first of December.

There was one hope, the high tide the next night would be, according to the book, almost as high as the one on which we grounded. If we got our big navy anchor out astern and buried it and brought the cable to our deck winch, and backed up with full engine we might pull free.

That night the wind veered completely around to the other side of the compass. Instead of blowing southwest it came up northeast, one of these savage northeasters that in winter pour out of our deep coastal valleys and fjords, out of the Skeena basin and the Portland Canal, blowing fifty, sixty miles an hour for days on end. The sky becomes clear blue, white clouds race across it and the temperature plummets to way below freezing. It was then that

The crab man.

we learned a fact of nature previously unknown. Southwesterly gales blow water in from the ocean and lift the tide level. There could be a difference of as much as two feet on identical tides under these conditions. That night we were all set to pull off, our big anchor planted astern with the cable on the winch niggerhead. But the *Ogden* just lay there like a stranded whale, she never even lifted her bilge off the ground.

If there is anything more uncomfortable than a deep-keeled boat heeled over on a flat shore I don't know what it is. The deck is at 45 degrees, impossible to stand on, one has to slide or crawl to get around. Our fo'c'sle bunks were on the high side and we had to nail them up with bin boards to keep from falling out. It was bitterly cold and our coal stove at this queer angle kept going out on us. We had little grub aboard, but for some reason we had a good supply of rolled oats which keeps the stomach from complaining.

My worst worry was how to get word to my wife, Jessie, in Masset, that we were safe. With the big gales on and no word from us since we left Ketchikan I knew she would be frantic with worry. We did have an idea that if we could get to the Triple Island lighthouse which was a few miles to the north and where there was a wireless, we could send word of our plight. We did get Fred's little boat going and tried it one day. Once we were outside the harbour we found the northeaster piling savagely into the Tree Knob group of islands, steep, freezing waves that tossed us about, our sputtering gas engine threatening to quit at any moment. We sensibly gave it up and returned to our stranded ship.

The next run of high tides would peak on the 15th of December but they would be lower than when we grounded. If we missed getting off then there would be no further chance until two weeks later. We had one shovel aboard. Fred was a genius at mechanical improvisation. He took an oil drum that we had aboard, cut out a piece of steel with a cold chisel, and made another shovel, crude but useable. We started digging. We lay on our stomachs under the bilge of the boat, digging under the keel, day and night, whenever the tide was out. Every once in a while the big boat would slide with a crunch a little ways into the hole we had made.

While this was going on there was no word in Masset of our survival or otherwise. Jessie was terribly worried. She had no money but she managed to borrow enough to send a telegram to the Customs House in Prince Rupert. At that time a boat going to the islands had to obtain a customs clearance. Customs wired back that we had cleared. My wife went for help to our Haida friends and as usual they gave all the assistance that they could. Their guess was that the *Ogden*'s engine had broken down and in the grip of the ferocious northeaster we had either blown out to the open sea or else we were wrecked somewhere on the north coast. Henry White took out a search party that looked for us along the north shore as far as North Island and reported that there was no sign.

Air-Sea Rescue in 1932 was a phrase not yet coined. But after ten days the Lighthouse Tender, *Birnie,* came out for a look and found us in our conspicuous but safe perch, and sent word to Masset that we were shipwrecked but safe.

On the fifteenth we were all ready. We had dug our ship down almost two feet. We buried a log, a "dead man," in the beach behind our stern and this time rigged a cable with blocks to get an extra purchase for the winch. The big tide came in at night, we had the engine roaring in reverse, the winch pulled mightily, and the *Ogden* never budged.

Desperate at the thought of spending Christmas and New Year in Squaderee we worked all the next day digging under the boat. We even put bin boards under the keel and greased them. The next night was our last chance. We went through the same performance, this time she moved, and we were afloat again, our boat back in its proper element.

At Masset I got Jeff White and a friend of Fred's called Walter to go with us to Naden. Each of us had a rowboat and a few rings. It was a miserable time of year to be fishing. The harbour was full of drifting ice. In the mornings we had to get the snow off our boats, bail them out and fasten the bait in the rings with freezing fingers. Somehow we got our days mixed up, we came into town for Christmas and found that we were one day too early. The crabs were coming good, we were so hungry to make some money that we even returned to Naden and fished on Christmas day, much to my wife's disgust.

From *Tales from the Queen Charlotte Islands: Book 2*

Simpson's crabbing career was not a money-maker. The enterprise folded in March 1933 and his two partners in Ketchikan owed him $60.00, which they were unable to pay. Twenty years later, however, he got a letter from one of the men, who was in Seattle, saying he knew he still owed Simpson $60.00 and if he was ever in Seattle he would pay him. Simpson and the long-suffering Jessie went to Seattle and had dinner with the partner, who then gave Simpson a cheque for $75.00. "It temporarily restored my faith in mankind," Simpson said.

A Lonely Holiday

by Reverend Charles Moser, O.S.B.
Copper (Tzartus) Island, B.C., 1877

For a year Father Nicolaye remained at Hesquiat with Father Brabant, or taking his place when the latter was absent in Namukamis (the winter camp of the Ohiat Indians in Barclay Sound on the west coast of Vancouver Island), building a church. When this church was built Father Nicolaye made his home here, taking charge of the six tribes of Barclay Sound, Nitinat and Pachino [Pachena]: "The Church was blessed on Christmas Day 1877, by Archbishop Seghers, and called St. Leo's Mission. Father Brabant had come also for the

The church at Hesqiuat.

occasion. But the buildings were not finished by any means. There was only a single board partition between church and house. For want of lumber no ceiling or partitions could be made in the house. There stood a bare chimney in the centre of the little dwelling, around which I could turn at will, chasing my own shadow. Or, to break the monotony, I would allow the dog, cat and goat to come together—and then we had a 'picnic,' a 'jolly good time,' running around the chimney.

"One of my experiences is that a man can bear almost anything (hanging I don't know, I never tried it) except to be weeks and months alone without any possibility of seeing a human being. I had to bear it because of necessity, but I must frankly acknowledge that those four months were the hardest I ever put in. In years gone by [and still in 1925] the natives had, as a rule, two camps, one for winter and one for the summer. The winter camp was generally in a sheltered nook of a deep inlet of the sea; the summer residences were outside, on the shores of the ocean. It was thither my natives went on the day following the blessing of the church, and not a soul was left behind on 27th of December besides myself, my dog, cat and goat."

From *Reminiscences of the West Coast of Vancouver Island*

First published in 1900, these reminiscences appeared in the *Messenger of the Sacred Heart* in New York, under the title "Vancouver Island and its Missions." The Reverend Jos. Nicolaye arrived in Victoria from the American College at Louvain in August 1876, and joined Father Brabant at Hesquiat "on trial" in September 1876. He later took charge of the new church at Namukamis in Barclay Sound until 1888, and then moved to Kyuquot where he lived from 1880 to 1890. The Reverend Charles Moser also served on the West Coast with Father Brabant.

Roast Stuffed Goose

One domestic goose, 7–11 lbs.

(Should be less than a year old or it may be tough.)

Preheat oven to 425 degrees.

Rinse cavity of bird and pat dry. Sprinkle cavity very lightly with salt. Stuff loosely with Apple-Raisin Stuffing (allow one cup of stuffing per pound of goose).

Tie legs together with string and prick goose all over with a fork to allow fat to escape.

Place breast-side up in shallow, uncovered roasting pan. When lightly browned, reduce heat to 325 degrees. Allow 30 minutes per pound cooking time. Drain off fat as it accumulates. Prick with fork several times while cooking.

Apple-Raisin Stuffing

1/2 cup butter

1/2 cup finely chopped onion

2 1/2 cups chopped apple

1 cup seedless raisins

1 teaspoon salt

2 tablespoons chopped fresh parsley

1/4 teaspoon fresh ground black pepper

1 generous teaspoon of poultry
   seasoning (or roughly equal mix of
   thyme, sage and basil to make up
   1 teaspoon)

dash cinnamon

5 cups soft stale bread crumbs

Hint: A wild goose is not nearly as fatty as a domestic bird. Rub skin of wild goose with 1 tablespoon seasoned flour. Roast as above but do not prick skin. Cover with strips of bacon, or baste frequently with apple cider, or equal amounts of apple juice and chicken stock.

Melt butter in heavy frying pan. Sauté onion for about 5 minutes, until just transparent. Add apple, raisins and seasonings and cook over low heat for 5 minutes.

Pour mixture over bread crumbs. Toss together well. Makes enough stuffing for a 7–8 lb. goose.

The Yule Log

by Eva Emory Dye
Fort Vancouver, Oregon, 1839

December arrived. Basil's Christmas fires kept up incessant roaring. The rafters of the provision house creaked under the weight of birds picked smooth and white. The high-backed settees took on a knowing air as Dr. McLoughlin walked through the kitchen. The tin and copperware winked on the wall. Even the kitchen had Christmas greens.

Burris set all his Kanakas in a whirl. Some turned the plovers on the spit. Some set the quails on the gridiron. Burris kept an eye on the sun-dial, and every now and then took a sly nip of ale behind the buttery door. With a thump of the rolling-pin he announced the Christmas dinner. Fat goose, cranes, swans, so fat they swam in grease, plum-duff crowned with holly, ducks, showing the rich red after the knife, and baked quails, white to the bone,—these the Oregon epicures ate for Christmas dinner in 1839.

The tables were removed, and the governor in flowing peruke and ruffled waistcoat led the dance with Madame. The hall blazed in greenery. The tall central posts were wound with holly-leaved Oregon grape, the Christmas candles were wreathed in ivy. A Yule-log of fir beaded with globules of resin snapped and sparkled. Scotch clerks and English kissed the pretty girls beneath the mistletoe, plucking each time a pale gray berry from the bough.

And who were the pretty girls? Eloise, of course, and Catherine—the Canadian Lily. Six weeks Ermatinger duly courted her; and then they were married. From the mouth of the Columbia there came the handsome Birnie girls, whose father, James Birnie, a genial, jolly Aberdeen Scotchman, kept the only hostelry from Vancouver to the sea and from Sitka to San Francisco. Old Astoria, renamed Fort George, had been abandoned; but after the Clatsop trouble Dr. McLoughlin had sent Birnie there to keep a lookout for passing ships. Here he cultivated a little garden, did a little Indian trading in salted salmon and sea-otter skins, kept a weather eye out on the bar over which at long intervals a ship came into the river. Astor's old post was burned; only the scarified and blackened chimney stood among the ruins that were overrun with brier and honeysuckle. The latchstring of Birnie's log house on the hillside was out to the trapper, the trader, the Indian, and the sailor. More than one old missionary has paid tribute to the housekeeping virtues of his pretty wife, the daughter of a Hudson's Bay trader in the north country. Her blazing hearth, clean-scrubbed fir floor, and neat pine table of snowy whiteness, offered cheer and comfort to all the early wanderers who came "the plains across or the Horn around." Sole Saxon of the forest, Birnie's flag was first to welcome the incoming ship, and last to wave a farewell from the shore.

Chief Factor Pambrun, the *tinas tyee* (little chief) that held in check the upper tribes, sent down his fair Maria, the pride of Walla Walla. Pambrun himself was a blond with thin light curls. This in his child developed into peach-bloom red and white, blue eyes, and the midnight hair of her mother rolling in her father's curls.

At this Christmas festivity, Douglas and his wife Nelia, Rae and Eloise, Maria and the clerks, and the Birnie girls and Victoire, the daughter of La Bonté from the valley, all whirled in the dance together. Dr. Barclay lifted his eyes to the unexpected beauty of Maria Pambrun "in her kirtle green and a rosebud in her hair." She danced with David McLoughlin. David's long, black locks had a careless grace; he had his father's fine, straight nose, and his mother's square-set mouth; there was a ring on his finger and a sword at his belt. Dr. Barclay's eyes followed the pair with a strange surprise, and David—cared for no one yet.

"Ah, I beg your pardon." It was unusual for David to do an awkward thing, but he trod on Bruce's toes, and Bruce had corns. Snuff-box in hand, the old Scotch warder reposed from the care of the flags, the guns, the garden, and the gate, sleepily watching the weaving dancers and thinking—of Waterloo, perhaps. Burris, portly and rubicund, resplendent in a huge roll of colored neckerchief and horn spectacles astride his nose, slipped out again—to take a nip of ale behind the buttery door.

To be the governor's guest at Christmas was no light honor. Monique and Charlefoux were there in their gayest dress, fine green cloth coats and silver buttons, crimson caps and golden tassels, cutting pirouettes and pigeon wings, stamping in the noisy rigadoon, and heeling it and toeing it on air. Tom McKay alone made no change in dress. With the free, frank manners of the Scot and the grace and affability of the Frenchman, he came in his hunting outfit. Scorning the effeminate foppery of the Canadians, he wore as usual his leathern belt, from which depended the powder-flask, the bullet-pouch, and the long scabbard that concealed the sword-like hunting-knife. Tall, dark and powerful, Tom McKay acknowledged no master save McLoughlin. No other man could do what McKay did at Fort Vancouver or on the trail. His name was a terror in the mountains. The Indians believed this Hudson's Bay cousin of theirs bore a charmed life; the whites knew him to be an unerring shot. But with all his fierceness Tom McKay had the gentle heart of a woman.

Past midnight the dance, half Highland with a dash of Indian, ceased, and the dancers disappeared. Old Burris returned in his peaked nightcap and carefully bore away the last brand of the Yule-log to light the next year's Christmas fire. And he took a nip of ale behind the buttery door.

From Christmas to New Year's, feudal hospitality reigned at Fort Vancouver. The servants' rations were doubled and they danced more madly. On New Year's every employee put on his best and mounted the flight of steps to the governor's door. Madame and her daughter stood at the heaped and laden tables, and with gracious air dispensed English candies, cakes and coffee to the governor's guests. . . . So ended the Oregon Christmas of 1839.

From *McLoughlin and Old Oregon: A Chronicle*

Fort Vancouver, now Vancouver, Washington, on the north bank of the Columbia River, was founded by Hudson's Bay Chief Factor Dr. John McLoughlin in 1825. Probably the most important settlement on the Pacific Coast until about 1845, the fort was in an ideal location, easily accessible by deep-sea vessels. It was a natural gathering place.

McLoughlin ruled supreme. Canadian by birth, American by inclination, McLoughlin was described as imposing, six feet four inches tall, with a fine, deep voice. His impressive mane of hair earned him the nickname of "white-headed eagle." At the Fort, officers ate from Spode china and enjoyed the finest food and wine and a comfortable lifestyle. McLoughlin's warmth toward American settlers caused problems with his Hudson's Bay Company masters. He retired from the Company in 1846 and moved to Oregon City, anxious to become an American citizen. McLoughlin died in 1857, aged seventy-three.

The Oregon Territory was created in 1848. Fort Vancouver was abandoned by the Hudson's Bay Company in 1860, after Oregon became a state in 1859.

Letter Home

by Edmund Hope Verney

The Small Bower: Esquimalt, V.I.
Christmas Day, 1863

My dear Father,

It is pleasant to think that they "miss me at home" and that somebody says "how sad to spend another Christmas without poor dear Edmund," and that a few weeks hence a letter will arrive from you, dated to-day, telling me what you are doing at this moment, 11:30 a.m. here, but about 7:45 p.m. with you, what toasts you honoured after dinner, who you[r] circle consisted of etc. Before my windows lies the "Grappler," the yard-arms and mast-heads adorned with bunches of evergreen, and a young fir-tree growing out of the funnel, while my porch and verandah are similarly decorated. I know that between each recurring Christmas we might more keep in mind the love of Our Heavenly Father which we this day

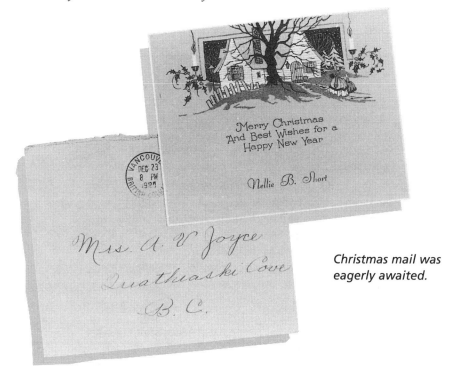

Christmas mail was
eagerly awaited.

54

celebrate. I rejoice greatly in having all your photographs, by which I bring you before me and think lovingly of you each on this day.

Dec. 26. This letter will be taken to England by Mr. Robert Burnaby: he is one of the principal merchants of Victoria, and greatly looked up to and respected: I have asked him to call upon you, because I can confidently recommend him to you as a man whose opinion is worth something: he is of the firm of Henderson and Burnaby, and a member of the House of Assembly: he is not such a young man as he looks, and if you are good enough to show him any little attention your kindness will not be misplaced: there are not many here of whom one can conscientiously and confidently speak as well: so many are either visionary or actuated by sordid motives in either praising up or depreciating these colonies, but I think Burnaby is sound and moderate. I have been reading the Bishop's speech at Salisbury, and I really could not endorse all he says about B.C.: although of course he has been all over Cariboo, while I only went a few miles up the country, and must speak a good deal from hearsay.

The serious winter has not yet commenced, although certain foreshadowings seem to indicate that it will be pretty severe.

Your affectionate Son,
Edmund Hope Verney

Burnaby takes home for me a little parcel addressed to you containing seeds for Mamma, and a marten skin for Aunt Fremantle.

E.H.V.

From *The Vancouver Island Letters of Edmund Hope Verney 1862–1865*

Edmund Hope Verney spent three years on Vancouver Island in command of a Royal Navy gunboat, the *Grappler*, during the Cariboo Gold Rush, when the population of Victoria almost doubled. Verney, who was actively involved in the social and legal affairs of the Island, carried on a lively correspondence with his father Sir Harry Verney, a prominent British Member of Parliament.

The Vanishing Turkey

by Hon. Dr. John Helmcken
Victoria, B.C., 1850

O h, the merry days when we were young! Turkeys were rare, but Dr. Trimble had a turkey which he kept on his premises on Broad Street. Daily he and Mrs. Trimble would visit his treasure, who with his fantail erect and feathers vibrating and with a gobble-gobble and proud step would show his pleasure at the meeting, but the doctor and wife, although admiring and loving the proud and handsome bird, had murderous thoughts in their "innards," and declared he would be a splendid bird by Christmas for dinner, so in due course they invited some half dozen friends to eat the turkey on Christmas Day.

A few days before Christmas, the doctor and wife, on their daily visit, found the turkey had vanished. Inquiries were made for it, and the invited friends were assiduous in helping to unravel the mystery, and concluded in the end that it had been stolen. They condoled and sympathized with the bereaved, and tried to assuage the grief by telling Trimble and wife that they would give him a

dinner on Christmas Day instead! The grief-stricken parties accepted the invitation, as the best thing to be done under the unfortunate circumstances. So on Christmas Day they assembled very jollily. The earlier courses were eaten with fizz, etc. Now comes up the principal dish, which being uncovered displayed a fine cooked turkey. Trimble was a good-natured fellow, so you may easily foretell what followed. Who stole the turkey? The echoes of their laughing, intertwining shadows reply "Who-o-o?"

From *Some Reminiscences of Old Victoria* by Edgar Fawcett

This book, published in 1912, is full of stories of early Victoria and how it evolved from a muddy fort to the jewel city of Vancouver Island. Many of the tales are written by pioneers whose names are familiar to us through street and park names.

James Douglas, governor of the colony of Vancouver Island, appointed John Helmcken Physician to the Provincial Jail in Victoria about 1851, a post he held for nearly sixty years. Helmcken was active between 1856 and 1871 in the affairs of the Island before the colonies of Vancouver Island and British Columbia became the united Colony of British Columbia in 1866. His general practice included Emily Carr's family. He and his horse Judy were well known throughout the streets of Victoria.

Spotted Dick
(Steamed Pudding)

1 cup of finely shredded beef suet (1/2 pound)

1 cup of light brown sugar

3 egg yolks

1/4 cup rum or brandy

1 cup raisins

1 cup of chopped dates

1 cup chopped walnuts (optional)

2 teaspoons grated orange or lemon rind

1 teaspoon ground nutmeg or ginger

1/4 teaspoon allspice or cloves

1 1/2 cups fine dry bread crumbs

2 teaspoons baking powder

3 stiffly beaten egg whites

Beat suet until softened, then gradually blend in brown sugar, egg yolks and rum or brandy. Add raisins, dates, walnuts, if desired, orange or lemon rind, and spices. Combine bread crumbs with baking powder, and add to suet mixture along with egg whites.

Put into well-greased mold. (A hinged pudding mold or large coffee can covered with several layers of foil and tightly tied with string, or any suitable covered container.) Molds should be no more than two-thirds full.

Place mold on a trivet in large pot or in canner. Steam must be able to circulate all around. Steam gently for about four hours. Allow to cool before removing from mold.

Serve hot with hard sauce, custard or whipped cream.

Brass Buttons

by Florence Goodfellow
Victoria, B.C., 1868

During the Christmas holidays some friends of my parents asked me to stay with them and I was asked to all of the Christmas festivities. The greatest event for the young people was a large Twelfth Night Ball at Government House. Oh, the wonderful joy of it! There were two men-of-war at Esquimalt and crowds of middies. My friends lived just over the hedge from Government House, their name was Stallschmidts, English people with two daughters of my age. We all went to the ball. I am afraid the poor young boys of the town did not have a very good time as the naughty girls had eyes for nothing but brass buttons that night. I was almost delirious with joy. It seemed as if it must be a dream. I went to so many parties through the holidays. It was a delight to write home and tell all about it. The postage was twenty-five cents a letter. I wrote once a week.

From *Memories of Pioneer Life in British Columbia*

Florence Agassiz was born in eastern Canada and came to British Columbia in 1862 with her family. Her British-born father, Lewis, "a dismal failure" as a farmer in Prince Edward Island, set off to find gold in the Cariboo, again without success. The family settled in Yale; Lewis became the chief constable and postmaster at Hope. The "jail," unused in its first role, became a chicken house and the family flourished.

After many adventures they settled in the Agassiz Valley, named for the family. Florence and her siblings made many visits to friends in Victoria, where she met Mr. Goodfellow of the Bank of British North America. They married and settled in Victoria.

Holiday Travel

by Charlie Taylor Sr.
Port Alberni, B.C., 1890s

The entertainment [. . .] was held in a large room over the Alberni Trading Company's store. And I think there must have been about seventy-five people there. I think everybody in the valley at that time attended. The concert started early and everyone joined in the dancing, singing and games. The music was supplied by Johnnie Drinkwater with his violin. Johnnie had just arrived from Ontario and had a real good selection of quadrilles, waltzes and other dance music at his fingertips. Kenneth McKenzie also played his violin and the late Jim Redford played the accordion. As far as I can remember there wasn't a piano or organ there. In those days it was the custom for everyone present to sing, recite or do something to entertain the rest.

I might say here that the transportation problem in those days was pretty hard and the guests arrived by various methods of travel. I don't recall anyone having a buggy or wagon. The few horses here were saddle horses and quite a few arrived on horseback. Mr. George Smith of Sproat Lake picked up the Sproat Lake people and the McCoy Lake people with his oxen and sleigh and took them as far as the old Company farm, where they were met and ferried across the river in a canoe by Dan Clarke, making the rest of the journey on foot. Mr. Harry Hills and Kenneth McKenzie both brought in the Beaver Creek people with their teams of oxen and sleighs. I was telling Ed how they used to make sleighs for their oxen in those days. First of all, they would make the frame with the cross pieces, then take two saplings, spring them into place and spike them down, turn the sleigh upside down and there were your runners.

I will, as far as my memory serves me, tell you of the entertainment and those taking part. First of all there was Captain Huff who sang several songs, mostly songs of the south as plantation songs were a favorite with him. [. . .] Malcolm Shaw, a real Highlander and a brother of Mrs. Erickson, did the Highland Fling, and he really could do it. Hector McKenzie and Mrs. Clarke, mother of the late Dan Clarke, danced a Scotch reel. Hector was wearing old Parkinson's hob-nailed boots and cut the floor up pretty badly. [. . .]

Then there was Billy Smith, or Cockney Smith, who I think was the star of the evening. I think that at one time Billy sang in the London Music Halls as he certainly had a professional touch.

This reminiscence is part of a December 26, 1946 interview by radio host Ed Cox, of CJAV Radio in Port Alberni, which is still broadcasting there. Charlie Taylor Sr. was one of the first white settlers in the Alberni Valley.

Santa's sleigh, drawn by reindeer, arrives at Pioneer Square, Seattle in 1907.

Laddie

by Lillian Bateman
Stillwater, B.C., 1920

December 24, 1920. Tomorrow would be Christmas, our first Canadian Christmas. Of necessity, it would be a simple one. Mother had already warned my brother and I that Santa might not find our little shack buried in the B.C. forest. Even if he did spot us, it was more than likely his sack would be empty by that time.

Sammy, not yet two, looked disappointed. He had heard enough of my stories of reindeer and flying sleighs to half believe in a real Santa Claus. At seven I knew better. Santa was only my Dad.

Mother looked down at our sober little faces and relented. "Well, you can hang up your stockings at least. There's always a chance that he'll find us." She paused, looked out of the window at the swirling snow. "In the meantime you'd better pray that this storm lets up or Daddy might not get home."

I went to the small window to see for myself. The heavy snow had fallen steadily all afternoon. Now all traces of a path had disappeared. It was growing dark and still there was no sign of Father.

Indoors, Mother and I had done our best to welcome him home. We had cut a lovely little fir tree to perfume the air, and had decked it out in all our old familiar treasures. True, the angel looked a bit tired, its tinsel dull and tattered. Our tiny red-felt Santa had definitely seen better days, but the strings of golden balls still glittered bravely as they reflected back the yellow lamplight. Most of them, in spite of our many moves, had survived. Where branches appeared too green and bare, Mother had placed bright old-fashioned cards, keepsakes from the Boston years. I had painstakingly cut and glued a red paper garland to drape around the lowest boughs. Then came the candles. As I carefully fastened their metal clips to the ends of the branches, I wished we could light them, just once . . . even one single, solitary candle. I asked Mother. I should have known better. It only started her on her stories about trees alight, houses burning, and children being destroyed.

Finally we were finished and stood back to admire the tree and discuss the stockings. We decided to wait until bedtime before hanging them up behind the heater. That was as close to a chimney as we would ever get in this place. Perhaps, I told my little brother, if Santa did come, we would find a nice red apple or an orange, maybe a handful of nuts and a striped candy cane in the morning. We might even get a real surprise. But of course, Daddy had to make it home first. There could be no Christmas without him.

All day our conversation had centered around Father. When would he arrive? What might he bring? Would he like our tree?

Now, with the snow still falling, we began to have doubts. Could he walk the six miles up from camp in this weather? Mother said she doubted it, not in such a storm, not in the dark. There were the trestles. I thought of the snow covering the slippery ties, and of the white water of the Eagle River far below. I began to hope he would play it safe and wait until morning.

Weekdays he worked in the big machine shop at the edge of the wharf in Stillwater. When he came home to visit, he tried to catch a ride up on the speeder or a late train, but tonight there would be no train. Everyone would have gone home early to be with family, or was off to Vancouver for a logger's spree. If he planned to get home tonight, he would have to walk, and it was a stiff grade every step of the way to the trestles.

A
MERRIE XMAS

It's sugar and spice
( ) and everything nice
I'm wishing for you today;
And enough Christmas cheer
to last a whole year
And make you glad, happy and gay.

Santa comes calling, circa 1930s.

Mother told us if Daddy left camp at five he would likely be home before ten at the latest. We ate a silent supper, our ears tuned to the world of snow outside, hoping to hear a footfall, a bang on the door. Sammy grew sleepy and was tucked into bed. Mother and I sat close to the heater, quiet, listening to the whine of wind and hiss of snow against the window. Ten o'clock came and went. I began to droop. Mother told me to go to bed. She put another stick of wood into the fire and resumed her silent vigil, wrapped in her private thoughts. She hardly heard me say goodnight as I kissed her cheek.

Suddenly, about midnight, there was a lull in the storm. The silence wakened me. I was lying listening to the quiet when I thought I heard a scuffling, shuffling noise, and a couple of solid thumps.

"Dad!" I screamed, and leapt out of bed, wide awake, my heart pounding. I was just in time to see a grotesque, snow-covered figure stagger into the room. A blast of cold air and a swirl of snow followed. He stood hunched over, puffing, quite out of breath, and stamped his feet about as if to make sure he was on a solid floor. So far he had said nothing, nor had we. We were awed by this figure and waited for it to speak. Abruptly he bent over, opened his Mackinaw, and a shapeless brindle bundle dropped to the floor. Now we were truly speechless. The object reassembled itself into a puppy right before our eyes. What a dog. A blond, brindled, flop-eared, black-muzzled creature with a rubber band for a spine. He wriggled, twisted, and contorted until his whole hide seemed to undulate. The rolling wrinkles came to an abrupt end at the stub of a tail he was trying so hard to wag in greeting.

By now Sammy had joined us. He rubbed his sleepy eyes; they grew rounder and bluer than ever. His mouth fell open. "A DOG!" he barely whispered, then, "Gee! What's his name?"

While Dad removed his wet Mackinaw and started to work at his boots, we all flung questions. "Where did you get him? How'd you ever get him home? How old is he? Did he have to walk in all that snow?"

Looking serious, practical Mother said, "Is he housebroken?"

Dad said the pup was about four months old; his name was Laddie; he was part bulldog, part Airedale; he was housebroken; he walked most of the way, but had to be carried over the trestles, where Dad almost lost him between the ties. Dad buttoned him inside his jacket most of the rest of the way home. The dog was getting played out and slowing him down.

Mother wanted to know how Dad got him, so he had to confess Laddie was given away by a fellow in camp who was going to "knock him in the head." Sammy and I gasped at this news, but Mother sensibly asked, "Why?"

By this time my brother and I were on the floor with the dog, sharing his wet kisses. Dad was still struggling out of his high boots. "Oh," he said, between puffs, "this guy has a kid, little girl about as old as Sammy here, and the damn dog kept knocking her down. The kid would barely get on her feet when Laddie here would run and jump on her . . . figured it was some sort of game. Anyway, this guy's wife said the dog had to go, she'd had enough of howling kids. Nobody at camp would take him, not with that habit. So, here he is. Guess I didn't like the idea of him killing the dog. That's it." He stood up, looked at Mother's doubtful face and then at Sammy, rolling about with the dog.

"We'll soon take care of that jumping-up business," he announced.

Now Sammy and the dog had begun to play. Laddie dashed off and sat on his haunches about eight feet away. He looked alert and expectant. Sammy had risen and was about to give chase when the dog launched himself at the boy's chest. Down he went and the dog raced by, turned, and sat poised for a repeat performance as soon as the child got on his feet. Right now Sammy sat red-faced and angry, his eyes watered but he didn't look like he was going to cry. He looked mad. He was slowly beginning to get on his feet when Dad intervened.

"Wait," he cautioned. "Now, take this." He placed the wire-handled, short, steel poker in the boy's hands. "Pay attention, now. Listen. Hold it like this, see? The next time Laddie runs at you, be ready, give him a good whack on the nose, see? Like this." He held the boy's hands around the poker and demonstrated. "That's all. Whammo."

Sammy caught on fast. Armed, he got up slowly, eyeing the dog all the time. His bright eyes had the glint of battle. Feet apart, he waited for Laddie to make his move.

Accepting the challenge, the dog ran, jumped . . . and suddenly the game took a new twist. The victim had stepped back and swung the poker across the dog's thick skull. For once he was the one to sit down suddenly. He stayed down, shaking his head and looking puzzled, watching the boy with the poker. Whatever he thought, no one knows, but he got the message. He had taken his last jump. You might think he would forget this lesson and return to his old tricks after a few days, but he never did. He was an intelligent dog. One whack from a small boy had solved everything.

He grew into a fine watchdog and playmate. It may have been a poor Christmas in some ways, but I remember it as the best ever. Laddie was the most exciting gift two lonely children ever received.

From *Forgotten Villages of the B.C. Coast: Raincoast Chronicles*

The Lamont family came from Seattle, Washington to an isolated cabin in Stillwater, B.C. Not surprisingly, Lillian Lamont Bateman reports that her mother "did not want to leave Seattle."

Hello! Santa Claus

Another consignment please of Xmas Fruits, Candies, Bon Bons, Fancy Crockery and Novelties, for our Christmas trade.

We are not excelled in Choice Groceries.

JOHNS BROS.,
Cor. King's Road and Douglas St.   VICTORIA.
Telephone 433.

Miners at Mass

by Edgar Fawcett
Victoria, B.C., 1860s

At Christmas there was the usual influx of miners from far-off Cariboo down to spend the winter in Victoria, with pockets well-lined with nuggets. It was "easy come, easy go" with them, and liberal were the purchases they made for their relations and friends.

Christmas Eve, after dinner, mother or father or both with the children were off to buy the last of the presents, visit the shops or buy their Christmas dinner, for many left it till then. Turkey might not have been within their reach, but geese, wild or tame, took their place. Suckling pig was my favorite dish. Wild duck and grouse (fifty cents per pair), with fine roasts of beef. Of course plum pudding was in evidence with poor as well as rich, although eggs at Christmas were one dollar per dozen.

A great feature of Christmas time was shooting for turkeys and geese at several outlying places, and raffles for turkeys at several of the principal saloons and hotels. The place I best remember was the Brown Jug, kept by Tommy Golden.

A special feature of the saloons on Christmas Eve was "egg-nog," and all we young fellows dropped in for a glass on our way to midnight mass at the Catholic Church on Humboldt Street. It was one of the attractions of Christmas Eve, and the church was filled to overflowing, and later on there was standing room only. [. . .] Amongst the well-dressed city people were many Cariboo miners—trousers tucked in their boots, said trousers held in position with a belt, and maybe no coat or vest on. When the time came for the collection, all hands dug down in their pockets and a generous collection was

Egg Nog

1 egg, lightly beaten
1 teaspoon sugar
1 jigger dark rum, brandy or other
　　liquor
4 jiggers milk

Shake vigorously with cracked ice, strain into an elegant, tall glass. Sprinkle with ground nutmeg.

the result. My old friend, Tom Burnes, was one of the collectors on one occasion. There were not sufficient collecting plates, and Mr. Burnes took his hat and went amongst the crowd who were standing up in the rear of the church. As he passed through a group of miners, friend Tom was heard to say, "Now, boys, be liberal," and the response was all that could be desired; for, as I said before, it was "easy come, easy go." "Twelve-thirty," service is over, we are off to bed, for we must be up betimes in the morning for service at 11 o'clock.

Hot Rum Toddy

1 jigger dark rum
1 teaspoon sugar
2–3 cloves
small piece of cinnamon stick and a dash of ground cinnamon
1 slice of lemon
dash lemon juice
ground nutmeg

Combine all ingredients except nutmeg in tall, heavy glass. Fill with hot water and sprinkle top with nutmeg.

From *Some Reminiscences of Old Victoria* by Edgar Fawcett

The collected stories in this book are written by people whose names read like a who's who of historic British Columbians. Politicians, newspaper publishers, lawyers and doctors from Victoria's early days comment on everything from the growth of the Post Office to the architecture on Wharf Street.

Christmas Day on a Warship

by John P. Hicks

Esquimalt Harbour, Vancouver Island, B.C., 1901

I wish I could tell you in "Jack's" own terminology just how the day is spent on board ship, but I cannot. He promised to write it for me, but failed to do so; but you seem anxious to know so I will give a brief outline myself with a few quotations from my man of the fo'c'sle as memory may serve.

First of all he assured me that "We shakes out about 5 o'clock and stow hammicks and go through the usual routine, you know; then we gets breakfast quarter to height; and after that there's 'Divisions.' "

This was going a little too fast for my purpose, but I had to let him go on and return for more details later, in fact, supply some from my mental notes taken on a previous occasion when I went the rounds with "Hurricane Bill." I may here explain, however, that "Divisions" is an invariable part of the daily routine, and means that at a certain hour, in answer to the bugle call, seamen, gunners, stokers, marines, come rushing up the gangways from all parts of the ship to "fall in" on the main deck for inspection. It really means very little, only to see that all hands are there, and in two minutes they are scampering back to their places as fast as they came.

"After this church parties fall in," my friend said, "just the same as Sundays."

"Yes, I understand that part of it," I said, "but what about your decorations, and mottos, and so on?"

"Auw, yes," he said. "We 'av a bit of decoration alright, but there's gener'ly one or two chaps detailed off for that, d'ye see, from each mess; we makes 'er look a bit nice, you know, sometimes, and fix around flags and buntin', and this wot-e-call paper—this thin stuff—different colors—you know what I mean— you get at the shops up town."

"Tissue paper," I said.

"Yes, sir, that's it. Then we 'aves a bit of mistletoe put up of course, and we brings out all the photos we've got of them ets 'ome, you know and put 'em round, and we gener'ly 've got a fair number, amongst us in a mess, you know—My word if we 'aven't."

These photographs are always among a sailor's greatest treasures, and he never tires of showing them to his sincerely interested visitors. And you would be astonished at the elaborateness of the decorations, so modestly referred to above, and the exquisite taste displayed. If you could see a mess on an ordinary day, then visit it again on Christmas morning you would not recognize it as the same place and would be amazed that such a transformation was possible. There is an ingenuity and an originality about the arrangement and designs such as only the inventiveness of the "handy man" could devise. I have sometimes wished that it were consistent with the convenience of the ship to maintain the homelike attractiveness of the Christmas Day mess throughout the year; but that would make the Navy too popular and—less effective.

By the time church parade is over the "cooks of the mess" have about completed their extra functions, and are beginning to let the galley cool off a bit. Everything is on the table and you can "smell a good taste" all over the ship. Presently "still" or "alert" is "piped" and "the rounds" begin. That is to say, all the officers of the ship (and often their lady friends with them) form in

Naval ships in Esquimalt Harbour, 1902. Lighthouse in background.
(Photographer Leonard Frank.)

procession, from the captain (or admiral if a flagship) to the boatswain or gunner, and headed by the band, go and make a call at every mess in the ship with the conventional wish of "a Merry Christmas." It is amusing enough to see the band, dodging up and down the gangways, and going single file through some of the narrow passages, and playing all the time; but there is fun too for the officers in the sights they see and sounds they hear. The tables are fit to tempt a king, with viands the most substantial and the most delicate. There is not only "roast beef and plum pudden" (or "figgy duff") but turkey and chicken and ham, with salads and sauces, and Christmas cake, and mince pie, with nuts and oranges and other fruits, and the rule is (which cannot be broken without giving offence) that each officer and friend must taste something from each mess table. Each officer, too, if he keeps his eyes open is liable to catch a suggestion of the esteem (or otherwise) in which he is held by the ship's company, for discipline is relaxed on that day, and men may express, in a good-natured way, by suggestive mottos hung in conspicuous places, and in ludicrously artistic designs, the pent-up and accumulated grievances of the year, without running the risk of punishment. Indeed, a shrewd captain often gains a clearer insight into existing conditions by that one round than he could do by any other means, and not infrequently changes are quietly inaugurated with the New Year looking to greater harmony and contentment. Often these mottos refer also to the service rations, which are certainly inadequate and sometimes unwholesome, especially the salt pork, and biscuit, which the "tars" often jocularly declare were first packaged by Noah when he entered the Ark, and have been in the British Navy since Nelson's day.

After "the rounds" are ended turkey and chicken disappear almost as quickly as if they travelled on their own pinions and shortly Jack prepares to go ashore. A "free gangway" is given, which means that all classes of men in the ship may go on "leave"—bad characters included. Don't inquire too closely where they go now. And if you find out don't blame the lads too severely until you ask yourself where else could they go? In Victoria at least, they could hardly go anywhere else for there is hardly anywhere else to go. You say "that does not excuse him." Of course not, and he is no doubt often a fool; but you and I, may be, are not without responsibility in the matter. Ought we not to provide some other resort for them? When this is done (and it soon will be) you may discover that "bluejackets" are not all "boozers" and that they are not without hearts and consciences which respond to kindliness and truth.

But I have written enough—more than I have made interesting, I fear, and I will stop with the wish—your wish and mine—of a Merry Christmas to—

> *. . . the sailor men*
> *That sail upon the seas,*
> *To fight the wars and keep the laws,*
> *And live on yellow peas.*

From *The Methodist Recorder*, December 1901

At the turn of the century, six or more warships of the Royal Navy Pacific Squadron were in Esquimalt Harbour at any one time. The ships, and their officers and men, were very much part of the Victoria scene, and the Royal Navy instigated most of the dances and social events. The biggest celebration was a regatta to mark Queen Victoria's birthday on the 24th of May. Most ships at this time were steamers, but some still used sails.

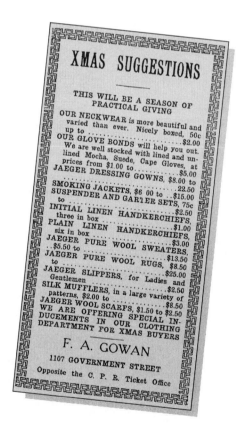

Crackers and Whiskey

by James Francis Tulloch
Orcas Island, Washington, 1875

My first Christmas on the island was rather a lonely one as I had made no acquaintances and books and papers were not to be had at all. I was amused at the manner in which Caines and Billy O'Donnell were celebrating it. They had a jug of whiskey and a box of crackers and they sat astride a bench and first one and then the other had to tell a story or sing a song and the other would treat, or vice versa and they kept this up till both of them fell into a drunken slumber.

From *The James Francis Tulloch Diary: 1875–1910*

Orcas Island is the largest of the cluster of the 170 or so San Juan Islands. Roughly midway between Victoria, British Columbia and Bellingham, Washington, the Islands form a bottleneck between the Strait of Georgia and the Strait of Juan de Fuca that accelerates the tidal flow in the narrow channels between the islands. Tulloch and his wife Annie had nine children, all of whom were born and raised on their Orcas Island farm.

Logger's Gastown Christmas

by Dr. W. Wymond Walkem
Granville, B.C., 1877

Burrard Inlet, so far as population was concerned, was a very small place in 1877. There were two mills doing business on the Inlet then—mills, too, that were renowned all over the world, even at that early period, for the quality of the lumber that they shipped abroad. These were the Hastings Mill and the Moodyville Mill. Both of these mills employed a large number of hands. [. . .]

At that time there were no hotels, or saloons, in Moodyville; but there might just as well have been, because there was one hotel at Hastings, kept by Maxime Michaud, a French-Canadian, who was reputed to be wealthy, and there the men obtained all the liquor they desired. [. . .]

In addition to the many employees of the mills living in their immediate neighborhood, were numerous logging camps, both on the inlet itself and scattered along the coast on the several timber claims belonging to the companies. Jerry Rogers had a large camp, for instance, at Jericho, where some of the finest timber that was ever cut was got out and towed by the powerful tug *Maggie Rogers* to the booms of the Hastings Mill. Angus Fraser had a camp on Bowen Island, and Furry and Dagget had another camp in what is now known as Stanley Park, removing some of the giant timbers from that now

Line drawing of "Granville in the Early Days"

famous reserve. This camp was the last of five different camps which at one time and another worked within its boundaries.

Scattered along the coast from the head of Johnstone's Straits to Burrard Inlet were the shacks of scores of handloggers who cut timber on their own account and sold them to the mills after they had been scaled by the mill scaler. These men were usually in partnerships of two. Some of their dwellings, or shacks, were located in most picturesque spots, and were often hidden in the dense foliage which surrounded them, and their locality could only be divined by the chutes they built, on which the immense sticks glided into the water. [. . .]

Most of these loggers led a very lonely life. There were very few steamers churning the waters of the northern coast in those days, except one or two bound for Alaska, or an occasional tug in search of some hand logger's boom, which was ready for the mill. Months might go by, and these men would never see a stranger. You may imagine therefore that they looked forward to Christmas time with a happy anticipation of fun and frolic. Those who were any distance away would take advantage of some passing tug, perhaps a couple of weeks before Christmas, and make their way to "Gasstown." They were, on the whole, a good class of men. Brawny and well developed, they were the finest of axemen. Those who arrived first in Gasstown usually spent the most of their time on the waterfront, keeping a sharp lookout for others who were expected from day to day. Every man was known, and it was a daily speculation with those already arrived as to whether Jack or Tom would be the next arrival.

Yes, it was good to see the welcome which each man received as he ran his boat up by the floating stage in front of Mannion's Hotel. All hands would go down on the landing stage until it would threaten to sink with all on board. Then the hand-shakings followed. Having moored their craft, they would be led up the bank—and the drinks that would go round, and the questions, and the laughter—all good-humored, and then the enquiries as to their prospects, and as to how much they had cut, and what their last boom had measured. Then out they would all go, and visit some other houses of cheer, until they had made the round.

And I am proud to add that there was little drunkenness among them. They drank, but they were not drunkards. They were a superior class of men to that. Ask Mannion, who is here with us today in Vancouver. He will tell you the same. Of course there were many among these happy fellows who never touched any liquor stronger than beer, and some not even that. The most of these men were of a saving character, and had money coming to them at the offices of the mill, and after spending Christmas in Gasstown would take a little trip to Victoria, which was at that time the Mecca of British Columbia.

When Christmas Day arrived, the hotels would all be full. The tables always groaned with the best the market afforded. Geo. Black made a point of having the finest of bunch grass beef for those who patronized him on Burrard Inlet. The dinner was the meal on Christmas Day, as it always is the world over, and these dinners in the hotels of Burrard Inlet were no exception to the rule. Yes, and the boys always had toasts, in which their lady loves were not forgotten. Joe Mannion and Capt. Clarke would sit at the heads of their respective tables with smiles broader than their countenances, and that they were not niggardly in any way was amply demonstrated at the close, for cheers for their hosts invariably followed. Then all would adjourn and play cards, or checkers, in the rooms allotted to those games.

Leaving the hotels of Gasstown, and paying a visit to the logging camp at Jericho, there you would receive a welcome spontaneous and hearty. Jerry Rogers was always proud of his Christmas dinners. They were high-class, and put on the table with great ceremony. Sometimes a miniature barbecue would be furnished the boys, as the old man affectionately called his workers. Such a dinner! Better than you can see in this city today. Venison fat and juicy— suckling pigs and turkeys (none of your cold storage turkeys either, but killed and dressed a few days before); ducks and geese, both wild and tame, and a huge sirloin of George Black's best bunch grass product. A monster plum pudding with a sprig of holly, and aflame with brandy, wound up the feast, to bind together what had gone before. Small stowage, Jerry called it. How the old man's eyes would twinkle as he watched the feast, and listened to the occasional sallies of wit which burst from different parts of the table. [. . .]

To give a proper touch to the feast, there were always two twenty-gallon kegs of beer on tap. The good old man was the happiest of the band, for to make his men happy at this festive time was his single aim. [. . .]

The other camps also commemorate Christmas Day after similar methods. There was the Furry and Daggett camp. This outfit was always celebrated for the excellence of their table, which was looked after by the wife of one of the partners. Angus Fraser, who had a heart as big as an ox's, made a special point of seeing that the Christmas dinner should be up to the mark. Being a married

A winter sleigh ride in Stanley Park, 1899.

man, his Christmas was partly spent in the camp and partly at home.

On both sides of the inlet, those who were not connected with the camps spent their Christmas much as they do now. Plum puddings and mince pies engaged the attention of the busy housewives for weeks in advance of the festive occasion. Isolated to a certain extent from the rest of British Columbia, a social and sympathetic feeling bound all as though in one family bond. Go into any house where there were children, and your ears were greeted with squeaking trumpets and hammering of drums, and even before you reached the door the evidence that Santa Claus had not forgotten the little children of this far western harbor was before your eyes in sleighs being pulled on sawdust and mud, or skates being tested on the same material. You often hear today of the high prices of eggs; but prices here today are low in comparison with the price of eggs in 1877. We obtained most of our eggs, turkeys, geese, ducks and chickens from an Irishman who paid occasional visits to Burrard Inlet with the fowl I have mentioned, and also with potatoes and vegetables, which might be in season.

Billy Paterson—that was his name—came from Semiahmoo, and did a roaring business here. He always managed to sell his whole cargo, which was carried in a 12-ton sloop. Just about Christmas time those with eyes bent upon the First Narrows would see this indefatigable trader making his way in on the rising tide. After clearing his sloop at the local customs house, Billy would make the round of Gasstown to ascertain how the supply and demand stood, in respect to the farm produce which he carried under his hatches. Eggs were always in demand at this period for making "Tom and Jerries," and good stiff prices were asked and paid for absolutely fresh eggs. In 1877 eggs were high— in price, I mean—and you could not buy them for less than $3.00 a dozen, and we were lucky to get them at that.

I have already told you that the little children were not forgotten at Christmas time. The population of the province was small and much scattered, and old Santa Claus had very long journeys to make, which necessarily took up much of his time. He always came to the inlet two or three weeks in advance of Christmas and took a good look at all the little boys and girls to settle in his mind what kind of a present would suit each one. As his sleigh was always full for little Indians of the northern missions, and as he had to make time, he always made arrangements with the captain of the *Etta White,* who was a distant relation of his—at least the captain used to say so—to bring up most of the presents from his storehouse in Victoria the day before Christmas, and also a special team of reindeer, small enough to make their way down the stovepipes which led into the houses. There were no chimneys, consequently he had a tight squeeze to get near any little child's stocking. But he was very good and never forgot any child. They were all well satisfied and well treated.

The effects of Christmas generally led up to a kind of ennui which lasted until over New Year's Day. Then the boys would begin to make a move towards their shacks, laden with all kinds of remembrances of their holidays. Let me add that many of the residents here spent their Christmas in Victoria or New Westminster. Some even went as far as San Francisco.

We had visitors, too, from New Westminster, as the sleighing was good in winter, and if there was not too much snow on the ice I think a good many used to find their way to Burnaby Lake, where they would enjoy themselves immensely.

When the Christmas week was over in old Gasstown the little burg went once more asleep for another year.

From *Stories of Early British Columbia*

Stanley Park, Bowen Island and Jericho were the main logging camps around the fledgling city of Vancouver. This story tells of groups of loggers and individuals who worked from floating logging camps along the coast. These camps flourished until the Second World War, and although some continued to operate after, this way of life has disappeared.

Wymond Walkem, the health officer for Victoria late last century, came to British Columbia about 1870. He collected and wrote stories of local people, which were published in books and newspapers.

The Logger's Winter

by George Fraser
B.C., 1906

When a heavy snow has fallen,
And the air is full of sleet,
Mid slush and fallen branches
You are searching for your feet;
When just before the daylight
You are crawling up the chute,
Your spikes a-sliding backwards
And you're mud from cap to boot;

When your understandings leave you,
And you sit down "good and quick"
On a splinter nicely pointed
And thick as a porridge stick,
You have the satisfaction
Of having made a start
To pay your winter lodging
And study the woodman's art.

To kicking in the early morning
When you hear the frozen bell,
To growl at the snow in the coffee
And consign the cook to—well—
To fight the fallen branches
And cross the fallen trees,
Cursing your own sweet folly
In mud that is up to your knees.

Giant spruce trees on the Queen Charlotte Islands dwarf an admirer, 1918. (Photographer Leonard Frank.)

Digging out graves for the skidway,
With mattock and shovel and axe,
Cutting roots as thick as a schooner
With ice dripping down on your backs,
Or fixing a log with a choker
While the signalman hollers "Ahead!"
It's then that you think of the bunkhouse
And wish yourself back in bed.

And then you remember it's Christmas,
And you think of the "doings" in town,
And your feet become colder and colder,
With an itch to pack up and go down;
And somehow the weather grows colder
And the mountainous forests grow wilder
When you think of those nine o'clock breakfasts
And scenes that are certainly milder.

So some "sprained an ankle" or hand,
Others get "cold in the chest,"
The truth is the whole camp agrees
That a "Christmas in town" is the best.

From *The Log of the Columbia*

Nothing is known about the author of this poem, published in the Columbia Coast Mission's magazine, under the auspices of the west coast diocese of the Anglican church.

HEAVY MAILS NOW THE RULE

The Vancouver Postoffice
Department
Commencing to Feel the Rush
Extra Clerks Put on

It has become perfectly evident to the officials of Vancouver postoffice that the majority of the citizens are in possession of plenty of spare cash. This conclusion has been arrived at after witnessing the enormous amount of mail matter and parcels which has been dispatched through the post the past week, to eastern Canada, to England, to the United States, and in fact to all quarters of the globe.

Letters to Santa are commencing to arrive, the majority apparently written in haste in cramped little fists. Smudges on the paper, large and black, are also prominently identified with the missives which are addressed to the old gentleman.

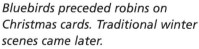

Bluebirds preceded robins on Christmas cards. Traditional winter scenes came later.

From *The Daily Province*,
Vancouver, B.C.
December 18, 1901

Ice Cream for Christmas

by Katie Walker Clarke
Campbell River, B.C., 1890s

Christmas when we were young was a wonderful event, looked forward to for weeks. We pestered Mother with questions to see if she could let us know for sure that Santa would really come! "Is the Mission chimney really big enough?" "I hope it will snow," said one. "I hope Santa doesn't get lost in the woods," said another.

Mother told us every year the old fairy stories about good old Santa; of course, he would come.

For Mother it was a busy time. There was extra cooking to do. She made nearly all our gifts, working until late in the night, so we wouldn't know what she was doing. Father, too, was busy as he made gifts (a sled for my brother and doll's crib for Winnie and me), but he could slip away to the cellar where he kept tools and material. His problem was Mother. What could he give her? Those early days were poor days, as money went. Nobody had much money.

The neighbours hadn't any money either, but they always found something to give even their neighbours. One neighbour who lived four or five miles away always

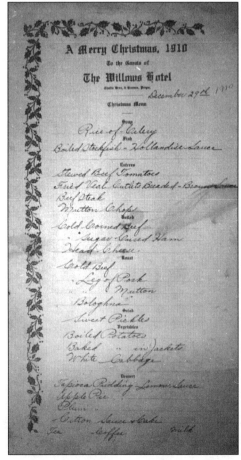

Christmas menu of The Willows Hotel, Campbell River, 1910.

gave us a goose. She raised them for Christmas presents for her neighbours and family. We never had a turkey for a long time, but the goose was wonderful.

Christmas! We were bubbling. Father was telling jokes. He always recited the Santa verses, where the "old fellow" and his reindeer drove up on the roof. Father was really dramatic when he had us for an audience. We could almost see Santa coming down the chimney.

We always had the "Bear" game; of course, Father was the bear and would chase us out into the cold hall. All this happened in the big warm kitchen where Mother was busy contriving something for a lunch.

If we had snow or ice around at Christmas, Mother made ice cream, a lovely boiled custard and cream. The method of freezing was far from modern. Father would bring in a big wooden bucket filled with snow and ice. He'd sprinkle it well with salt. Mother put the custard in a five-pound lard pail.

Then they packed the pail in the snow right to the top and twisted it back and forth in the snow or ice. We used to help, but little arms soon tired and Father finished it. We were all served a little dish before we went to bed. "Just a little serving Daddy. We will have the rest for dinner tomorrow."

While we made this delicacy last as long as we could, Father recited, with much drama, "Horatius at the Bridge." I don't know why I always demanded that story, I loved it in spite of the results of the battle. I always enjoyed history and still do.

With Horatius having done his duty to "fathers and gods," we hung up our stockings at the big fireplace and went to bed.

From *Musings*, November 1984

This reminiscence by Mrs. Clarke, a long-time resident of Campbell River, appeared in *Musings*, the newsletter of the Campbell River and District Museum and Archive Society.

Sunbeam

by Reverend Thomas Crosby
Fort Simpson, B.C., 1874

In the midst of the rush of church and mission-house building, Christmas came upon us. Preparations for the celebration, the practising of Christmas carols and the placing of Christmas decorations, had been going on for weeks.

We had been teaching them that Christmas was to be a time of peace-making, of love and of joy; and they got the idea, partly from the influence of the mission at Metlakatla, that all the quarrels and misunderstandings, and even their financial obligations, were all to be settled before the day came, which was to commemorate the birth of Our Lord the Saviour. On this account we were busy with great councillings, and the settling of disputes of all kinds, night after night, often until midnight.

Christmas Eve came, and the air resounded with the songs of the carol singers as they went from place to place throughout the town, singing the sweetly beautiful old time melodies which the missionary's wife had taught them.

As a preparation for the occasion every path through the place, among the large [. . .] lodges (there was only one shingled house outside the fort, besides the new little mission house just completed), was lined on both sides with evergreens, and along the rough bridge from the main shore to the island. Every imaginable kind of lamp or lantern was brought into use for the general illumination, and in many of the houses a dish with a little oil and a rag in it added its share to the brightness. Large fires were burning all night, and perfect order and quiet throughout the entire village was demanded by the council while the singers went their rounds.

The old people sat around the great fires, waiting patiently until the singers came, and they said "we were listening to the songs of the angels."

As the early morn came on, the old nurse went out from the mission house, where the first little white babe had been born but two days before, and returning, brought into the room with her the noble old chieftess. The missionary, fearing the results, had warned his wife not to permit them to come

Elaborately carved entrance to a Chief's house near Port Simpson.

in to see the little one. But the persuasive appeal of the nurse on behalf of "Su-dalth," the great chief woman, prevailed, and she was admitted into the room and put up her hands in astonishment before the mother and the wonderful baby.

By this time there was great excitement throughout the village, people were moving from house to house shaking hands with everyone, expressing their good will, and wishing one another a happy Christmas.

No sooner had the old lady returned with the news that she had seen the little white child, when a string of human beings started up the hill to bring their greetings to the missionary and his wife, and satisfy their curiosity. As one in such high rank had been allowed to enter the room, it was impossible to prevent the others without showing partiality, and so one by one they were permitted to stream in one door and out of the other, shaking hands with the mother and seeing the baby. As you may guess, it was something of an ordeal, but fortunately neither mother nor babe seemed to suffer.

Immediately after this, eleven o'clock service was announced, and all the villagers repaired to Chief Skow-gwate's house on the island. This large building, similar to the one shown in our cut, was crowded. Four windows were placed in it for light, two in front and two at the back, something of a variation from the old-time arrangement; the roof was covered with bark, and an immense crest pole stood at the door, representing the clan of the chief. We had a delightful service, the singing being led by Mrs. Morrison, wife of Chief Factor Morrison at the Fort, and her brother.

The afternoon was spent in feasting, little family gatherings, where reconciled friends met. These occurred among the more Christian part of the community. One man told me he had attended fourteen parties; it certainly spoke volumes for his ability to store away provisions.

In the evening a magic lantern exhibition of scripture views was presented to the intense delight of hundreds of people.

Next day, still keeping up the festivities, the whole village was invited to a feast in Chief Suk-say-uk's house, the missionary among the number.

After they had partaken freely of the food, speeches were made by the chiefs and leading people, telling how joyful and happy they were that they had seen that day. At the close of the speech-making, they began to clap their hands and cheer merrily, when the missionary, not having yet learned their language, asked what it meant, and they replied, that they had been looking through the records of their people for a suitable name for the missionary's daughter, and as he was now to be connected with La-ge-uk's (the King of the nation) tribe, the name of his little daughter was to be A-she-gemk, and they cheered again.

On again making enquiry as to the meaning of this name, he was told that it meant "leg of the sun or moon," or freely interpreted, "Sunbeam." This we added to her English name Jessie, and as such she has always been known: "Jessie" to us, and "Sunbeam" to them. Jessie Sunbeam. However many happy Christmas times may come and go, there will be none more brightly pleasant to our memory than our first Christmas at Fort Simpson.

From *The Western Methodist Recorder*, December 1899

In 1874, Methodist missionary Thomas Crosby was invited to Fort Simpson (just north of what is now Prince Rupert) in northwestern B.C. by the Tsimshian people. Initially much respected by the Native people, the changes that Crosby introduced to their way of living were also his downfall. Although the Tsimshian adopted many non-Native ways, they were frustrated at not being accepted as equals by the white society. The Native people wanted to take part in the expansion of Fort Simpson, which by the 1890s was becoming important as a stop for ships bound for northern B.C. and Alaska.

Crosby's health deteriorated and in 1896 he requested a transfer. He left Fort Simpson in 1897 when he was appointed chairman of the British Columbia Conference of the Methodist Church of Canada. He had been at Fort Simpson for twenty-three years.

A Surprise Guest

by Melanie Mayer
Skagway, Alaska, 1897

Edith's life in Skagway that first winter was certainly different than the mild winters she had been used to in Tacoma. Although Skagway is protected by mountains on either side of Lynn Canal and its climate is moderated by the water, it has plenty of snow and below-freezing temperatures. And the winter winds, gathering force as they are funneled up Lynn Canal, can pack a real wallop by the time they reach the beach at Skagway. It was this, in fact, which gave Skagway its name, for "Skagua" was an Indian word which referred to a very windy place, one where the same air is never breathed twice. "[Skagway] was in the woods, you know, and the trail rode down and around. . . . We kids weren't very big, . . . and the wind blowed so hard that when we come out to the river bank, the wind would get a clean sweep and pick us right up and flop us right down on the ground! It was really rough!"

The Christmas of 1897 was a happy occasion for the Feeros. They had a snug, warm cabin and enough money to live comfortably. Prospects for the new year looked even brighter. The Christmas season also produced some surprises.

"In early days, they used to set the table, . . . then you covered it with a big cover. Grandmother made us a cover for the table, and she embroidered a little mouse in one place. And she said, 'That's my place at the table. I can't come because I get so seasick.'

Christmas dolls: Two little girls in Tacoma, Washington play under the tree on Christmas Day, 1899.

She couldn't even go on a boat tied up at the dock! 'But that's my place at the table. I'll always have a place at your table.' So when the table was set, Grandmother's place was put there too.

"So this Christmas, we had our Christmas dinner and had just about finished dinner when somebody raps at the door. My Dad went up to the door, and this fella stood there. . . . He walked in, and saw this place at the table hadn't been used, so he sat down and ate his dinner! When he got all through dinner, he said, 'Well, I suppose you folks are wantin' to know why I came for. I came to tell you we're having a Christmas tree downtown, and we want you to bring your children and come down. There's a law against vile shirts or neckties. You'll be fined if you wear one of those! But bring the children and go down.' So we did. Turned out to be the garbage man, when we found out who it was!"

That Christmas party was the first of many such community celebrations. It was held in the newly built, all-purpose Union Church. As was typical of the early days, entertainment was spontaneous and "home-grown."

"Went to the church, and church program was just about anybody. If you was there and could sing a song, well you'd get up and sing a song; if you had a little piece, then . . . , just anything you could do. That was our entertainment. We had the Christmas tree. The Christmas . . . program was about half over when Willie got sick!

"Mother said, 'You stay with the children. I'll take Willie home. He's a big boy now, and I won't be afraid to go home.' So they start out, and pretty soon in she comes, plowing in in a hurry! And she says, 'I'm not going home! There's some drunks up there!' They came out of the saloon as she was passing by, and 'Why-ya whoop!' and fell off the sidewalk! She turned and ran. She was scared to death. But you know, Willie wasn't sick anymore that night."

From *Klondike Women: True Tales of the 1897–98 Gold Rush*

John Feero got as far as Skagway in his journey to seek gold in the Klondike. He realized he would arrive too late to be able to stake a good gold-bearing claim, so he settled in Skagway and sent for his family. Twins Edith and Ethel, whose recollections are above, were his daughters. Feero ran a successful business packing goods over the Chilkoot Trail, but in the course of his work he developed a hernia. Feero planned to go outside for an operation when, caught in a snowstorm, he died of pain and exposure in December 1898. His family remained in Skagway.

Presents and Poker

by Florence Tickner
Maud Island, B.C., 1930

The Christmas holiday season was always a family affair. The boat day before the big event was terribly exciting. Mysterious parcels arrived, and all our special groceries: Japanese oranges, green and black olives, celery, Brussels sprouts and hard Christmas candy. If money wasn't too tight there would be Christmas crackers, cranberries, candy canes, sweet potatoes and maybe even a turkey.

One year, Mom's brother Gordon (Uncle Bunt), his wife Charlotte (Aunt Lottie) and their five children came for a few days at Christmas time. It was a wonderful time for us children, who seldom had any others to play with. We went fishing, crabbing and clam digging, played board games and cards and had all sorts of fun. Every night we went to bed exhausted but happy. Mother and Aunt Lottie had a wonderful time too. Instead of being alone, looking after their large broods of children, they were together doing chores with one another, and their work seemed lighter because of it. The men too found the change very enjoyable. They cut wood, hunted deer and ducks and talked logging to their hearts' content.

Four days before Christmas, Dad went duck hunting because the budget didn't include turkey. He came home all smiles with ducks galore—bluebills, butterballs, whistlers and teal. The next day we all got busy plucking ducks. We had a great system: my oldest sister Shirley picked one duck, then started cleaning them while the rest of us carried on with the picking. Every once in a while we got a reject from Shirley. She made us work pretty hard getting rid of all the fuzz and pinfeathers. Picking ducks was usually our job, but once in a while Mom and Dad helped too if there were a lot of ducks to pick. Believe me, after two or three ducks, little fingers got tired and stiff, especially if the weather was cold.

A couple of days before Christmas the men went out to find a suitable tree. They brought three home for Mom and Dad to choose from—she was hard to please. There were, however, a lot of trees to choose from.

Buckley Bay sawmill on Queen Charlotte Islands, 1918.
(Photographer Leonard Frank.)

On the day before Christmas, Mom and Aunt Lottie kept us so busy we didn't have time to get into any mischief. We helped break bread for stuffing—imagine using that wonderful home made bread for stuffing! Mom popped some corn for us, and we strung popcorn on strings with some cranberries in between for the tree. There was some last-minute wrapping of presents too, and that was no easy task. Can you imagine trying to find a private place in a three-room house with thirteen people in it? In the evening we decorated the tree and put our presents under it. Mother always teased us by looking for all the parcels with her name on them, then shaking and squeezing them. This Christmas it was even more exciting, with all the people around watching her and trying to stop her. Then it was time for a Christmas story or two and, depending on our ages, bed. The older children were allowed to stay up a little later, as long as they were quiet, while the adults had a drink or two and finished wrapping presents, or played poker. We younger ones were put to bed in good time, but it did take a while to settle down. There were three girls at the head of the bed and two boys at the foot, so naturally the whispering went on for some time.

The sleeping arrangements were really something. Aunt Lottie and Uncle Bunt slept out in the storage shed but probably didn't mind because they got to sleep in a bit in the morning. In the house, as soon as one person woke up everybody was awake.

On Christmas morning, things got started very early. We had a rule in our house that breakfast had to be finished and the dishes all done before any presents could be opened. But if we had Christmas stockings, they were fair game, and we had fun with those. A couple of nuts, three or four hard candies, a small toy and a Japanese orange kept us busy for a while. Breakfast over, we opened presents with wild abandon—Dad by the tree acting as Santa. Our presents were simple and practical, but each one was a treasure to us. A colouring book and new crayons were received with enthusiasm, and we took pleasure in new books to read. We loved to get jigsaw puzzles too, as they were fun for the whole family. Toy handguns, especially cap pistols, were also popular—being on floats took nothing away from our enthusiasm for playing cowboys 'n' Indians. After all the presents were opened and we had played for a while, it was time for a light lunch—"not too much, and don't dirty too many dishes, because there will be lots more later on." Mom and Aunt Lottie then started on the dinner preparations, and the men made themselves scarce. We children worked on our puzzles and played with our new toys while the vegetables were prepared and the ducks were stuffed. Around four-thirty in the afternoon, when Mom opened the oven to check on the ducks, the aroma that filled the house was almost more than we could bear. When dinnertime finally arrived and the ducks came out of the oven, no one there would have given a thank-you for turkey. With duck gravy, mashed white potatoes, sweet potatoes, carrots, Brussels sprouts, stuffed celery and one stuffed duck for each of us, we had as good a Christmas dinner as anyone could possibly wish for.

After the dishes were done, six balloons were blown up in preparation for our game. We lined up on each side of the kitchen table and batted the balloons back and forth, not letting them touch the table or the floor. Aunt Lottie was stationed at the end closest to the stove and got most of the attention because it was great fun having a balloon land on the stove and burst. She would holler and bat it out of the way most of the time, but occasionally she missed. There was yelling and laughing going on, interspersed with loud bangs from popping balloons. It was a good way to shake down our large dinner, and we children loved it. When the last balloon popped it was time to settle down and the adults' turn for fun. The chairs were put back around the table, the gas lamp was pumped up again and they prepared for a lengthy game of poker. We were allowed to watch, sitting next to someone and "bringing them luck," as long as we kept our mouths shut. We got real good at it because bed was the only other alternative.

When people talk of the good old days, I choose to remember times like these: families together, enjoying themselves and being thankful for all their blessings.

From *Fish Hooks and Caulk Boots*

This story gives a feeling for the way loggers and their families lived along the coast during the twenties, thirties and forties. Float camps or floating villages were scattered among the fiords and moved from place to place in search of stands of tall, straight trees. Some loggers lived alone, others with their families, and still others in groups of up to twenty. In the larger camps there was often a cookhouse and bunkhouse, as well as individual homes. The family camp in this story was near Maud Island, at the entrance to Knight Inlet.

The Christmas Ships Came Sailing In

by Elisabeth Hakkinen
Haines, Alaska, 1920s

During the summer months, freighters of the Alaska Steamship Company brought tourists and freight to the isolated communities along Alaska's Inside Passage, and took away canned salmon, shrimp, and crab as well as people. Some of those people into and out of Haines were Army personnel and their families being transferred. In December more freight came into the ports than went out, and there were few tourists, but the Christmas ship brought one very important passenger—Santa Claus.

To alert the children for the arrival of this important personage, the Alaska Steamship Company, whose ships plied the waters of the Inside Passage for many decades, would alert their local agent of Santa's approximate time of arrival. The visit of the Christmas ship was always timed for a schoolday afternoon, even if the ship had to stop and wait somewhere in a hidden cove.

The agent would get word to the school principal, who in turn would let the teachers know, who would warn the children to put on extra warm clothing. It was about a mile from school to the dock, which was at the Army Post, Chilkoot Barracks, adjacent to Haines. Lacking snow-removal equipment, the road along the shore was unploughed. To make walking

Elisabeth Hakkinen on the Chilkat River in 1935 with the snow machine built by her husband. Powered by a converted motorcycle engine driving a propeller, it ran on ice skates.

easier for little legs, a number of the soldiers stationed at the Post would walk or snow-shoe back and forth along the road, tramping down the deep snow. These soldiers, stationed at the only regular Army Post in Alaska between 1922 and World War II, also performed this road "ploughing" service for many social events in both Haines and Chilkoot Barracks when the snow was deep in winter.

From the moment the ship was first spotted, its rigging and masts ablaze with festive lights, to its arrival at the dock, took about half an hour, almost the same amount of time it took the children to walk from school to the dock. A crew member would escort the excited little visitors, nearly a hundred of them, to the Forward Social Hall. It would be beautifully decorated, and Santa Claus himself would be sitting there, a large box full of wrapped gifts on each side of him. One side was gifts for the boys and the other for the girls.

Santa came all the way from Seattle, stopping at all the regular ports of call. If anyone asked him if he was real, he'd offer to let them pull his beard, which was definitely real. That convinced us.

The ship's musicians, usually a trio of piano, violin and flute or saxophone, played Christmas carols for us, and we children sang for Santa Claus. For the adults—teachers and some mothers—Santa dispensed big branches of holly and sprigs of mistletoe, both unavailable in Alaska.

As well as a gift, the children received apples, oranges and candy. Some would take their gifts back to school to open together. Some would hurry home with them, although some couldn't wait. As they trudged back in the darkness of an Alaskan winter's afternoon, the children's flashlights shone like a mobile string of Christmas lights, a sight probably appreciated by Santa and the ship's crew almost as much as their efforts were appreciated by the children.

This personal reminiscence was told to me by Elisabeth (Sheldon) Hakkinen. She was born in Skagway and grew up in Haines, Alaska. Mrs. Hakkinen took part in this special celebration of Christmas for many years—as a schoolchild in the 1920s, as a teacher in the 1930s and as a mother in the 1940s. The Alaska Steamship Company operated along the coast between about 1890 and 1950. Mrs. Hakkinen now lives in Oregon, but continues as Historian for the Sheldon Museum and Cultural Center in Haines. The center began with her parents' collection of Tlingit artifacts and pioneer memorabilia.

Christmas Visitor

by Izo Arima

Ikeda Bay, Queen Charlotte Islands, B.C., 1913

After devoting my days to hunting, Christmas came. The morning of the Christmas day Mr. Ikeda asked, "Would you take some Christmas gifts to the people in Jedway." He handed me three different parcels. I started climbing up the steep hill to cross the mountain to get to Jedway, carrying the big bag on my shoulder. In spite of the usual December weather, Christmas day turned out to be a beautiful day. The sun was shining brightly in the sky. The path on the mountain was very steep and hard to walk. I climbed up taking step by step, gasping for breath. When I reached the top at last I was sweating all over. I sat on a stone and took a big breath. When I gazed in front of me there was nothing but the continuation of the dense forest. There was no wind, no bird, no bear but just myself. It was absolute silence around me. I thought that this stillness was the very one which was said to be the death of all the creatures. I wondered if there existed any other place with such stillness in the world. My heart was filled with deep emotion.

Jedway is at the bottom of the hill. I said to myself, "Let's keep going." When I got to Jedway I didn't see anybody around. It was just like Ikeda Bay as the mine operation was closed.

I stopped at Thompson's first. He was the caretaker of the mine and they knew me as they had visited Ikeda Bay a few times before. As soon as Mrs. Thompson saw me at the door she ran towards me, saying, "My boy" and she embraced me with her arms which were just the same size as my thigh. I thought I was going to suffocate as she weighed more than 200 lbs. and I had never been embraced by a woman that size.

She was in jolly spirits and she said, "Please come in. Please sit down," putting her hand on my shoulder. She brought Christmas cakes and some fruit to me. She was so happy that she kept touching my cheeks and hair. I felt I was treated like a little boy but I thought that was because they didn't have any children. Her husband kept smiling. I left a Christmas gift for them and went to the next house.

The next house I visited was Prescott who was the police officer. They were also delighted with my visit. Mrs. Prescott ran into the kitchen and brought me some food. She said, "This is a home-made abalone pie." She said, "This is also home-made wild berry wine." The pie and the wine were delicious. When my face became red after having wine, Mrs. Prescott laughed and said, "You got drunk." Mr. Prescott was also in high spirits. I gave them a gift and left their house.

The last house I visited was MacFee who owned the hotel. She was a widower of 34 or 35 of age. She didn't have any children either. She was a very good looking lady. She was also very delighted to see me. Since there wasn't anybody staying at the hotel, she took me to the dining room. She said, "It's almost lunch time." And she cooked fried eggs for me. She sat down and started talking to me. She talked as if her lover was visiting her and her conversation didn't seem to stop. I wanted to listen to this beautiful woman's story but I noticed the time. I excused myself as it was getting dark, and I handed a gift to her. She said, "I got some freshly baked bread for you to take." She wrapped up the bread and handed it to me.

I stepped outside and thought about why they were so excited by my visit. My conclusions were simple, and I was rather sympathetic toward them. It might be because of the isolation and their not having children or not seeing people around them.

When I returned home Mr. Ikeda said, "Thank you for all the trouble. You must have charmed them with your fine character and they must have been very happy to see you. I am cooking Christmas dinner. We will have duck in substitute for a turkey." It was a good Christmas dinner.

From "Four Years at Ikeda Bay," *The Charlottes: A Journal of the Queen Charlotte Islands*

Izo Arima was a young Japanese man who worked with Arichika Ikeda from 1913 to 1917.

Ikeda, born in 1864 in Japan, was an adventurer who turned his hand to many things in his lifetime. He studied medicine and farming in Japan, came to America and worked on a California farm, preached Christianity, organized a labour movement and, at one point, tried to bring Japanese immigrants to Mexico. He searched unsuccessfully for gold during the rush to the Klondike. Back in British Columbia, he decided there was a market for fish fertilizer and so built a ship and sailed north in search of fishing grounds. He arrived in the Queen Charlottes and, in 1906, discovered copper at Moresby Island.

John Boots

by Reverend C.M. Tate
Bella Bella, B.C., 1902

John Boots was the village crier at Bella-Bella; not that he was hired to do the village weeping, when there was anything to cry about; but because he was the village messenger, sent out to invite the people to the feasts, when such functions were held,—which was almost daily. Indeed, at certain seasons of the year, six or eight feasts daily was quite common, and on such occasions John Boots was kept quite busy.

We do not know how he came by his name, although it may be assumed that it was given him by some of the Hudson's Bay Company officers, who occupied Fort Millbank, in the early days [. . .] no doubt some of those early traders had noticed that John Boots was the general servant, especially of the chiefs, hence they gave him this appellation, which belongs to a gentleman's under valet, on account of his work,—brushing clothes and cleaning boots. Or, it may have come to him on account of peculiar dress, which was very popular in early colonial times, namely, a tall silk hat, a H.B.C. three-point blanket, and a pair of top boots. But, be this as it may, when we arrived on the scene, it was plain "John Boots" wrapped in a blue H.B.C. blanket, and minus both silk hat and top boots.

Now, a feast of any kind was a matter of great importance to John Boots, for was it not his business to carry invitations, and see that all the guests attended, if they were to be found; but, a Christmas feast was something out of the ordinary, yet he determined to do his part faithfully in making it a success.

On one occasion when Chief Humchit was giving a feast to the leading men of the village, John Boots went from house to house, and opening the door he called out in a sing-song tone: "Chief Humchit is preparing a food and (naming the person invited) is requested to be present." But Chief Waukosh was not to be found, although John Boots searched the village high and low. No one knew what had become of Waukosh: he had not left the village, for his canoe was on the beach: neither was he at the store, for John Boots had been there twice to make enquiry for him. The only place he had not visited was the mission house; so off to the mission house he went, and entered without knocking, according to Indian custom. He searched the dining-room, the sitting-room, and the study; and was on his way up the stairs when we heard him. To our enquiry as to the object of his search, he replied, "Waukosh must be here, for he is not in the village." This persistent spirit served a good purpose, when the first Christmas feast was held.

The Indian style was to be laid aside, and the feast was to be after the white man's idea. Instead of sitting on the floor, and eating off the mats, tables were to be put up; and instead of the long wooden dishes, nothing but genuine crockery was to appear on the table. A number of young men were detailed as waiters; and the best cooks among the women were to make bread and buns, cakes and pies, sufficient to feed the whole village; and, lest there should be any lack, the Missionary's wife made a double portion.

When Christmas Eve arrived all the arrangements were completed, and about the hour of midnight a band of young converts went out from the mission house, and sang through the village, that never-to-be-forgotten song of the angels, "Glory to God in the highest, and on earth peace, good will toward men." After a few hours of sleep the church bell rang out the invitation, to "worship Christ the new-born King." [. . .]

At the close of the service, the invitations were orally delivered to John Boots, when he was charged to go to every house in the village,—not forgetting the white man who kept the H.B. Co.'s store,—and invite every member of every family, in each house; for there were five or six families in most of the houses. When he returned we asked him if he had remembered the old, and the halt, and the blind, to which he replied that those people were dead, and could not come,—meaning that on account of their infirmities they could not get

there without assistance. Then we sent him back to bring them; and he went away mumbling to himself that this was a new order of things, when the women, and dead people were invited to a feast. But he was equal to the occasion, and went first to one house, then to another, stirring up the bundles of rags under which the old people slept, telling them to arise and shake themselves, for they must all go to the feast. All were astonished, some protested, and others said he was jesting; but John Boots helped them to their feet, and led them one by one to the banquet house, and made them comfortable.

When all the guests had arrived John Boots was despatched to the mission house to tell the Missionary and his wife that the people were all seated, and waiting for them. We immediately followed the messenger, and when we arrived we found the great Indian house filled with guests; and, seated at the head of the table was a gentleman dressed in the uniform of a man-of-war captain, with epaulets and brass buttons, white collar and cuffs, well barbered hair, and waxed moustache. In the dim light we couldn't make it out: we looked out of the door to see if there was a war vessel in the bay; and when the guests saw our confusion, they shouted with laughter, which confused us still more,—until Chief Humchit came and introduced this great personage as the old Indian fire-tender, who generally sat in the ashes by the side of Humchit's fire, clad in an old grey blanket. The young men, to give us a surprise, had scrubbed the old man clean, trimmed his hair, and dressed him in this suit of cast-off clothes.

We took our place at the table, and [. . .] all enjoyed their first Christmas feast with glad and grateful hearts; John Boots, meanwhile, doing his utmost to make it appear that all the enthusiasm and happiness were due to his efforts; for, said he, "There could have been no feast unless I had brought the people together to eat it."

From *The Methodist Recorder*, December 1902

According to the journals of William Fraser Tolmie, the Dr. Tolmie mentioned in the story, the Bella Bella of today was the location of the Hudson Bay Company's Fort McLoughlin in Milbanke Sound in 1833. The fort was abandoned in 1843 and burned, but a Hudson's Bay store was erected later and the community became known as Bella Bella. Fort Millbank of this story is presumably the same place.

A Union Bay Christmas

by Janette Glover Geidt
Union Bay, B.C., 1906

Christmas, in the past, was the biggest celebration of the year. It seemed that the weather was always cold and the ground covered with snow. Everyone remembers sleighriding down Russell's Hill all the way to the wharf trestle, or down McLeod's Hill and negotiating onto the Government wharf. With cold wet mittens and pants, the boys and girls scampered home to a toasty kitchen, full of the aromas of shortbread and gingerbread. If they were lucky they could sample the goodies before they were stored away in old cracker tins. Poring over the catalogue, the children dreamed of an "Eaton's beauty" or a shiny red wagon. [. . .]

In 1904, Mrs. Cook taught Sunday School and had a big Christmas tree decorated with cookies for the children. The best part of the wonderful party was the gingerbread man that each child took home.

By 1906 the new church had been built, and Christmas parties were held there. A delegation of ladies travelled to Cumberland on the train and purchased presents from a fund of $80 which had been collected.

Attendance was so large at the Christmas Tree Entertainment that standing room only could be had. The large tree was prettily draped and ornamented. Its branches were fairly loaded down with presents for children, and even a few getting into their second childhood were remembered. The house was fairly brought down when one of our leading bachelors, who has scarcely a hair on his head, was handed a wig.

Family presents were often homemade from Mother or Father's workshop: a sturdy red sleigh, mittens, doll clothes, and cloth doll. Not wrapped, some gifts were stuffed, along with nuts and a "Jap" orange into the sock that had been hung before bed. Japanese oranges were imported before the turn of the century. In 1921 a box was $1.10, but by 1936 they were down to 59 cents a box. The box was wooden with many uses.

Fraser and Bishop had a good selection of gifts to choose from, but a trip to Cumberland was a must, even just to window shop and dream. Special presents

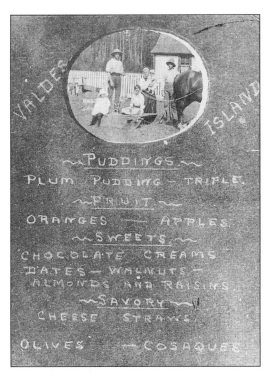

On the image menu:

PUDDINGS
PLUM PUDDING — TRIFLE.
FRUIT
ORANGES — APPLES
SWEETS
CHOCOLATE CREAMS
DATES — WALNUTS
ALMONDS AND RAISINS
SAVORY
CHEESE STRAWS
OLIVES — COSAQUES

Photograph of Bagot family on Christmas menu. Valdes Island was renamed Quadra about this time to avoid confusion with Valdez Island farther up the coast.

were ordered from the catalogue. For many years the Sunday School sent the ages of all its students to Woodward's or Eaton's, and the personal shopper selected appropriate gifts and mailed them back. In later years, when the younger people had money to spend, they loved to do their shopping on Christmas Eve at Fraser and Horne's, as the shelves contained many interesting items, something just right for each member of the family. [. . .]

But more important than the presents were the family get-togethers, with lots of delicious food. Mrs. McKay with her daughters and daughters-in-law prepared dinner for about forty-five in the large farm house. Two turkeys were stuffed and cooked in the oven of the huge coal and wood stove. Mountainous quantities of home-grown vegetables were boiled. Cranberry sauce made from berries picked in the summer at Fanny Bay was opened along with pickles and relishes. Dessert was plum pudding with hard or lemon sauce, or rich dark Christmas cake topped with almond paste. Two long tables were set in the dining room for the adults, with the youngsters sitting at the kitchen table.

The Glover families, although smaller, also got together. Each end of the long dining room table held a big "Tom" which Harry and Herbert, wielding Sheffield knives, carved, reserving the parson's nose for themselves.

The only time we ever had turkey was Christmas, and again at New Year's. It was the most expensive meat at that time, I think about 85 cents a pound. It would be bought with its feathers on and innards in. I think it was at least dead.

—Margaret (Glover) Matthews

Any festivity at the Glovers called for music. Every Christmas morning Harry sat down at the organ, pulled out all the stops, and woke the family with a rousing chorus of "Christians Awake, Salute the Happy Morn." Meanwhile Herbert was in his home playing the same piece on the piano. Carols were always enjoyed at night.

Since children grew up and often married within the community or district, both sets of parents expected the young family home for Christmas dinner.

For years we walked up to Grandma and Grandad Bowdens and had a huge turkey meal for lunch, then walked along the tracks for another turkey dinner at Grandma and Grandad Glovers. I think they all came to our house for New Year's dinner, more turkey. Guess it's good we didn't have a car and had to walk.

—Jacqueline (Glover) Gordon

The New Year was celebrated by groups of friends "first- footing" on New Year's Eve. This custom originated in northern England. For good luck, tradition demanded that the first to enter the house in the New Year be a dark person. This "first foot" was to carry a lump of coal in one hand and a bottle of whiskey in the other. The revellers walked and sang through the town, knocking at all the doors. They were welcomed in with a plate of Christmas goodies and a round of drinks. Needless to say, as the night wore on and more homes were visited, the "first-footers" began to stagger and their voices to slur. More than one could not face the delicious turkey dinner served the next day.

After the Community Hall was built, New Year's Eve dances were held with balloons and noisemakers at midnight. Tickets were sold out early, as people from all over the district wanted to be part of the fun.

From *The Friendly Port: The History of Union Bay, 1880–1960*

These recollections are set in Union Bay near Courtenay, once a bustling terminal from which Cumberland coal and coke were shipped around the world. Little remains of the operation but overgrown rows of ovens, which once operated around the clock to remove the natural gases from coal, to produce coke. Coke burns hotter and with less smoke than coal. The Geidt family recently returned to live in Union Bay.

Memories of Sea Otter Cove

by Monica Rasmussen

Cape Scott, Vancouver Island, B.C., early 1900s

There were no luxuries or treats, but we were never hungry. There was always a good garden, and salmon were easily caught. These were canned or salted and smoked. I can close my eyes now and smell the cool, damp scent of the smoldering alder wood in the little smokehouse. Meat was scarce, for game had been cleared out by cougars; and there was not enough open land in our area for cattle forage. We seldom saw butter. For a substitute, we rendered lard, added salt and pepper and a bit of onion for flavor.

For Christmas, we usually got a book or a game each; but best of all was our stockings, with peanuts in the toe, a Japanese orange, an apple, and homemade candy. We spent hours prior to Christmas helping to make candy holders from little match boxes—saved especially throughout the year for that purpose—and garlands from the colored pages of Eaton's catalogue, folded into strips, and pasted into links. They looked quite gay hung in loops across the room, and we thought they were wonderful. I remember, too, Mrs. Peterson showing us how to make tiny pincushions and glue them into half walnut shells, with a bit of ribbon to

An early Christmas card from the Campbell River Museum's collection.

hang them with; and how to paint faces on blown eggs and tuck them among the branches of the tree to grin merrily down at us.

There was always a community Christmas tree and dance in the Lake Erie hall, and everyone contributed something to make it a success. The bachelors in the settlement cut a huge tree for the center of the hall. It reached from the floor to the ceiling, and was decked with tinsel and tiny winking candles, which were lighted just as Santa arrived. To us little folk it seemed to go right up to the heavens.

From *The Cape Scott Story* by Lester R. Peterson

Monica Rasmussen was an original member of the small group of Danish immigrants who settled at Cape Scott, on the northernmost point of Vancouver Island, about 1897. The Danes were attracted to the New World by the opportunity to own land for farming, and by the rich fishing grounds literally on the doorstep. But lack of roads and transportation, the shipwrecks, storms and fog isolated and gradually eroded the spirit of the industrious settlers. The clincher was an announcement by the Government of British Columbia, just three years after the colony had been settled, that no new leases would be granted, and most of the original colonists had left by 1907.

As a centennial project, in 1971, the old eighteen-mile trail between Holberg and Cape Scott was cleared. Although rough, it is passable for those who wish to see the wild beauty of this historic area of Vancouver Island.

Christmas on Nelson

by Karen Southern
Nelson Island, B.C., 1918

Christmas was particularly dependent on the steamers. Although the pick of fresh-scented trees was at their doorstep, the steamer brought the trimmings for the festive season, the nuts and fruit, the cakes and Christmas pudding from home-folks, the cheerfully wrapped gifts, the newsy letters and the colorful Christmas cards. The grocery box from Woodwards was promisingly bigger before Christmas and sometimes protesting turkey crates were tossed down from the imposing steamer to the waiting boats rolling in the winter-gray waters.

Exciting were the Christmases when aunts, uncles, and cousins were also unloaded through the freight doors to swell the Christmas table and add to the general gaiety. The Hammonds almost always had visiting relatives who enjoyed the cordiality of the holiday runs on the steamers. The coal oil lamps on the *Chilco* and the *Chasina* lit up their brass clocks, wearing festive holly wreaths in their white-linen dining salon. A fresh-coated steward served the locally famous Union Steamship pound cake and seasonally garnished pudding. The captain and officers were more friendly than usual and made a point of showing the wheelhouse to the visiting children. A party atmosphere could be felt by everyone.

Christmas day at the Hammonds was a happy, busy event as all the bachelors in the neighborhood joined the family for a dinner of roast goose. In the center of their living room stood a huge fir with flickering candles clipped to its thick branches. The bright candles were magical in the soft glow of the lamplight and cast pretty reflections on the glass ornaments. Strings of red cranberries and puffed popcorn looped the bright greenery. After dinner the Hammond children and their cousins would join hands and dance around the tree merrily singing the yuletide favorites. A blazing fire warmed the room, and the spirit of loving and giving warmed those within.

And so Christmas was spent in Hidden Bay, snug in their home, insulated from the winter frost or occasional snow—or more likely, the lashing rain that

Union Steamship Christmas card. These ships were the lifeline along the coast for more than sixty years.

Christmas, with its floodtide of memories and its joyous manifestation of friendship and Goodwill, is our most cherished tradition. The personnel of the Union Steamship Company of British Columbia heartily wish you a Merrie Christmas and sincerely hope that your voyage through the New Year may be bright and cheery.

so often accompanies coastal Christmases. But one Christmas stood out from the others in Clara's memory as the year she lost her belief in Santa Claus. Santa in his red wool suit and white cotton beard, was reaching for a present from the tree when his arm brushed too close to a candle and his suit was aflame. At once, May had him wrapped in a rug, and when the fire was properly smothered, she unrolled poor Santa to reveal Cliff! The youngest Hammonds stared at their brother in surprise, learning the secret of the jolly old man the hard way.

Sis Harris' Christmas memory is a Veda doll hanging on the tree in the early 1918 morning. Her mother had bought the small glass doll, and carefully dressed it with homesewn clothes. Sis' brother had taken a pithy wood which he used for making whistles, and had run a hot wire through it, then threaded it with waxed string to make a tiny swing. They fastened it on the tree and sat the glass doll on it to surprise nine-year-old Sis.

Thelma Deberri (nee Johnstone) remembers one year that the steamer didn't cooperate in bringing the Johnstones their Christmas parcels until very late. For some reason, either the weather or the unusually heavy freight unloadings, the boat steamed right on past the regular island stop both going up and coming down the run. It wasn't until it went up and back again, that they finally unloaded their holiday ware. All that time the Johnstone Christmas turkey had paced its crate, gobbling half-heartedly, getting thinner and more seasick with every roll of the steamer. [. . .]

But the turkey or goose wasn't always the dinner fare for the big day, many had a roast of venison, and the Harding boys remember a depression Christmas dinner of stuffed cod wrapped in bacon, cooked by Paul and Bert, and enjoyed by all.

In fact, what went on the table often set Island Christmases apart from mainland ones, for it wasn't unusual to have dishes of steamed clams and oysters with melted butter, tasty crab legs, tender mussels, baked red snapper, and smoked salmon, to be tasted by all who visited. And they all visited, in fish boats and clinkers, by oar and sail, whatever would float and take them through the icy spray.

From *The Nelson Island Story*

Nelson Island was named for the British naval hero. Many islanders worked at the quarry where the famous Nelson Island granite came from. This stone was used in the Parliament Buildings and sea wall in Victoria, and in many other B.C. buildings.

A Savary Celebration

by Gladys Bloomfield
Savary Island, B.C., 1920

All the holiday supplies arrived on the Union boat, so had to be ordered well in advance. There was always a Christmas tree, put up a day or two before Christmas, decorated with ornaments and pencil-sized candles in metal clips, placed carefully so there was no branch above the candle which might catch fire. There would be green branches above the pictures and doorways, Christmas cards on the mantle, and accordion-type paper garlands looped to the corners of the room, and the lovely evergreen aroma of Christmas everywhere.

Early Christmas morning I would find my stocking hung on the foot of my bed. I could investigate this any time I wished and eat the first Japanese orange of the season, which it contained, but must stay in bed until the day began. The first order of business was to get dressed and repair to the kitchen for breakfast—and no fair looking under the tree en route! Then we would do the dishes and by this time Dad's fire in the fireplace would have warmed the living room so we could enjoy our tree and presents in comfort. Then we would visit our next door neighbours, the Maces.

There were always three big holiday meals. Mr. and Mrs. Keefer had the Christmas dinner, New

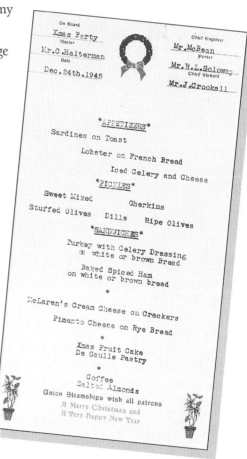

Union Steamship Christmas menu.

Year's was held at the Mace residence, and halfway between it was dinner at the Bloomfields. Late Christmas afternoon would find us walking down the road to the Keefers' house. If there was much snow we would walk along the beach if the tide would allow it. There were Christmas crackers to open and silly hats to wear and lots of anticipation while we waited for our plates and not much conversation as we appreciated our dinner. [. . .]

It was quite an undertaking to prepare for one of those dinners and to find a way to seat all the guests, for some of the summer people came to the island and we usually had 25–30 people. Long tables were made of planks on sawhorses, covered with sheets and tablecloths. Often chairs were carried from house to house to ensure adequate seating.

New Year's dinner always featured a beautifully cooked ham as well as turkey. Later in the evening we would go out to Mace's front porch or yard with all manner of pots and pans and other noisemakers to celebrate the arrival of the New Year, the object being to make enough noise to be heard in Lund, with a similar competition going on over there.

From *Savary Island News*, reprinted in *Sunny Sandy Savary*

Gladys Bloomfield lived on Savary Island for seven years as a small child. She recalls that when it snowed on Savary at Christmas, and when she was there it often did, the walk to the Keefers would be in single file. Her father had gumboots and led the way, then her mother walked in his footsteps, and then little Gladys. "He was careful not to take long steps," she says.

Rich Pound Cake

Preheat oven to 300 degrees. Grease a 10 x 5 loaf pan and dust with flour.

In a large bowl cream 1 cup butter. Gradually add 1 cup berry sugar and 1 teaspoon vanilla (or almond extract). Beat by hand or with beater until light and fluffy.

Beat until thick and lemon-coloured 5 large egg yolks. Gently add to creamed mixture and beat for four minutes.

Beat until stiff 5 large egg whites. Fold gently into creamed mixture.

Blend or sift together 1 3/4 cups all-purpose flour and 1/4 teaspoon mace. Gradually add dry ingredients to egg mixture, folding in thoroughly. Beat for two minutes by hand or at low speed with electric mixer.

Pour into prepared loaf pan. Bake in 300-degree oven for 60 to 75 minutes.

The Christmas Tree Potlatch

by Doris Andersen
Quadra Island, B.C., 1921

The government decided to step up its rate of prosecution of Indians who broke the Potlatch Law. [. . .] The great "Christmas Tree Potlatch" of Dan Cranmer of Alert Bay touched off the series of trials that ended potlatching forever for the Cape Mudge Indians and lost them all the potlatch regalia and valuable coppers which symbolized the wealth and prestige of the Lekwiltok.

It was just before Christmas, in December 1921, that Daniel Cranmer gave his potlatch, one of the largest, in terms of wealth given away, in Southern Kwakiutl history. It was held on Village Island, the home of relatives of Cranmer's wife, to escape the notice of the Indian Agent. Cranmer said: "People came from all over, from Lekwiltok to Smith's Inlet. The invitation was given to all the chiefs of all the tribes. . . . Three to four hundred men, women and children turned up."

"Hamatsa" and other dances were given the first evening. The second evening Chief Assu of Cape Mudge gave Cranmer the rights to a dance with shells and the right to several names. In return, Cranmer gave Assu a gasboat and $50 cash. The list of Cranmer's gifts to guests is staggering. It included

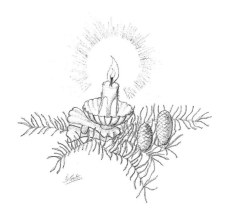

24 canoes, pool tables, violins, guitars, four gasboats, dresses, shawls, bracelets, 300 oak trunks, sewing machines, button blankets, 400 Hudson's Bay blankets, 1000 basins, glasses, washtubs, teapots and cups, bedsteads and bureaus, 1000 sacks of flour and sugar. Money was also handed out to adults, and small change thrown to the children.

"Everyone admits that that was the biggest yet," Cranmer said later. "I am proud to say our people [Nimpkish] are ahead, although we are the third. So I am a big man in those days. Nothing now. In the old days that was my weapon and I could call down anyone. All the chiefs say now in a gathering, 'You cannot expect that we can ever get up to you. You are a great mountain.' "

Treachery, however, attended the potlatch. An Indian constable was helping the dancers with their preparations, but secretly taking notes after each part of the performance, which lasted several days. Names and activities of all the participants were listed, and the notes turned over to the Indian Agent. Virtually all the Southern Kwakiutl were involved in one way or another. Sergeant Angerman of the Royal Canadian Mounted Police made arrests, and over 80 Indians were summoned to appear in court, some of them people of the highest standing in the Kwakiutl system, including Chief Billy Assu. Lawyers came from Vancouver to defend the Indians at the trial, which took place in Alert Bay in early March, 1922. The court consented to the lawyers' plea that chiefs who agreed to surrender potlatching paraphernalia and give up the practice should be released, and the Indians were given a month to make their decision. [. . .]

Chief Billy Assu called a meeting of his people when the ultimatum was given. He told them it was useless to continue the fight to retain the old customs. Some protested; they had debts to pay, and a future without the

pageantry and social significance of the dances looked bleak. To many of the older Indians who could not read or write, the idea of a substitution of legal papers for public announcements at the potlatch was meaningless.

But the threat of prison sentences was daunting, and few wanted their chief to suffer the indignity of imprisonment. "Assu had great respect from everyone. Prison would bring shame to him," explained nonagenarian Louise Hovell of Cape Mudge. There was resentment at the relinquishing of these family heirlooms, but almost every family surrendered its treasures as ransom for the chief.

From *Evergreen Islands*

In 1884, the federal government amended the Indian Act to make it illegal for Native people to hold or attend a potlatch. Missionaries along the coast deplored these ceremonial occasions, which lasted at least several days, since children missed school, adults were absent from work, and the practice of amassing wealth to give it away ran counter to the white man's way of steady work and saving. Potlatches were still held, but in secret. In the 1920s the government decided to reinforce the Act, and make an example of any Native people who participated in a potlatch.

Rather than surrender his potlatch regalia, Chief Dan Cranmer elected to go to jail, an action that made him a hero in the eyes of his people for standing up to the government. Some of the confiscated items were returned in the 1980s, and are now displayed in museums in Cape Mudge and Alert Bay.

Sorrow and Joy

by Reverend John Antle
Aboard the *Columbia*, 1929

I arrived at Englewood on Saturday, December 22, to join the *Columbia* for two weeks of intensive Christmasing, and to relieve Skipper Godfrey, who was about to take a well-earned holiday in Vancouver.

The ship was all ready for action. Dr. Stringer's hospital looked more like the toy department in Timothy Eaton's store than a hospital. Cartons of Christmas things from all parts of Canada, especially from Victoria, were stored in tiers on and under the cots, and it required all the doctor's knowledge of navigation to reach his dispensary. Cecil Fitzgerald, the *Columbia's* engineer, had assumed his usual role of Santa Claus, and was busy sorting presents, according to long lists of names acquired on the rounds during the year.

Everything was ready, even the usual stiff southeaster. However, the *Columbia* could not be delayed on such an occasion, and away we went for Echo Bay, a floating village where enough children were congregated to have a school and teacher. Mothers and children were on the *qui vive* and soon were assembled, together with women and children from Scott Cove and Simoon Sound, in the *Columbia's* cabin, in the corner of which a gaily decorated tree, properly secured for stormy weather, sparkled forth its welcome. Soon the ringing of the ship's bell and the tooting of the whistle announced the approach of Santa, with his bags filled with

Firmly secured—a Columbia *Christmas tree.*

presents, not only for the kiddies, but for grown people also. Sweets and oranges being distributed, Santa retired amid cheers, good wishes and invitations to come again.

A sudden metamorphosis, and he returned as a movie operator, in the person of Cecil Fitzgerald. Pictures were soon flashing on the screen, little, deeply interested eyes were staring, and nothing could be heard but the hum of the machine and an occasional yell of delight as the clown out of the inkwell performed some funny trick, or Bobby Bumps made a marvellous escape from the flashing sword of the Sultan of Turkey. Then, tired and all sticky, home to bed, not a long way, as the *Columbia* was tied to the floats on which the village rested.

Next morning was Sunday. The cabin, having been cleansed of orange peel and sticky sweets the night before, was changed into a chapel, and the chaplain, Mr. Govier, held a Christmas service for the whole population. Sweet child voices joined in the singing of Christmas hymns and grave little faces gazed with deep attention as Mr. Govier told the old, old Christmas story. The sun came out as the congregation left, and the ship steamed away to the next place.

In the woods tragedy always lurks behind the big trees, and we had scarcely got away from the joys of Echo Bay, when we ran plumb into a nasty accident. Sunday afternoon we called on a lone coast dweller, Mr. Wright, of Greenway Sound, who has a little boy, Doddie, 4 1/2 years, born at Rock Bay Hospital, and an ex-patient of Alert Bay. Knowing his mother was away, our visit was to give the kiddie a little Christmas surprise. It was all over, the kiddie all "lit up" with excitement, had gone ashore with his presents, and the *Columbia* was gathering speed for her next engagement, when a small launch was observed approaching, waving a flag of distress. Weigh on the ship was checked, and the launch containing one man came alongside. Briefly, an accident had occurred in a small camp miles up the Sound, and would we come. The launch was left behind, and with the young man on board, the *Columbia* set out at full speed for the camp. On the way we got particulars of the story.

The camp consisted of three men and two horses and was situated on a small platform, 1000 feet up from the water. The hillside was so steep that a man well "caulked" could with difficulty reach the top. The boss of the trio was in Vancouver, and only the teamster and the young man were left to run the camp.

That afternoon the teamster harnessed his horses to draw in a load of wood, and crossing a ravine the bridge gave way, and horses, load of wood, and man were precipitated into the ravine below. The man was pinned down by one horse, and his head lay in line with the heels of the other, and for one long hour he lay with five ribs and a leg broken trying to avoid the iron-shod hooves of the dying horse. In this he was only partially successful, as his cut and bruised face and head showed. Had he lost consciousness for a minute he would have been kicked to death, a contingency only prevented by the arrival of the only other man in the camp, who managed to get him out of the ravine and into his shack, which fortunately was not far away.

Then another difficulty confronted them. How to get him down the hillside. It would take four men, and there were not that number in Greenway Sound. Also there were to be considered the teamster's wife and little boy. So the young man climbed down the hillside, started the little launch and set out for the nearest neighbor. It was then that he saw the *Columbia* heading out of the Sound, and began to shout and wave his flag of distress. "Say," he said, "I haven't cried since I was a baby, but when I saw my signal answered, I let go. Oh boy! It was good to see her stop! Gee whiz, we're lucky!"

Dr. Stringer went up the hillside and fixed the man up for the night, and in the morning a party of four went up and brought the injured

A 1907 Christmas card featuring the vessels and mission hospitals of the Columbia Coast Mission.

man down to the *Columbia.* It took just an hour to make that thousand feet. Back again to the hospital at Alert Bay we went, left the damaged man to the ministrations of Dr. Watson, his wife and child in the hands of the nurses, and once more steamed off on our Christmas route.

After that it was a rush. Christmas tree and moving pictures from place to place for two solid weeks, giving seventeen "shows," involving 26 places, and covering 910 miles.

Towards the end, tragedy again stepped in. We arrived at Hardy Bay to hear the sad news that two young people, Leonard Davis of Port Hardy, and Geraldine (Jerry) Darrock of Blunden Harbor, had set out in a launch from Blunden Harbor to go to Hardy Bay. They had not arrived at their destination. Queen Charlotte Sound was thoroughly searched by motor boats, and later by aeroplane, but nothing was discovered, save the wrecked launch; and hope for their safety had been abandoned. Only four days before, Miss Darrock, full of life and a picture of sturdy youthfulness; was on board the *Columbia,* attending the Christmas tree and picture show at Blunden Harbor.

So it is with the dweller on the coast, and, as I suppose, elsewhere—sorrow and joy are always in the procession.

Toiling, rejoicing, sorrowing,
Onward through life he goes.

From *The Log of the Columbia*

Reverend John Antle, a keen sailor, first explored the practicality of a mission boat serving the B.C. coast by sailing his homemade sixteen-foot boat 500 miles from Vancouver to Alert Bay and back in 1904. He took his nine-year-old son Victor as crew. Upon his return, he convinced the Missionary Society of the Church of England of the need for a mission boat.

With a $2,500 grant, the *Columbia 1* was built in Vancouver at Wallace Shipyards on False Creek and launched in the spring of 1905. The Columbia Coast Mission was born. Its many boats and people would steam thousands of miles up and down the coast until the mid 1970s. Reverend Antle retired in 1936.

Christmas Cabin

by June Burn
Waldron Island, Washington, 1932

By now we had a living cabin, a study, a barn for the cow with a lean-to for the calves. We still wanted a cabin for the boys and one for Farrar so that every member of the family might have a private retreat. Farrar never built his own cabin but what fun we had building one for the boys. It was to be their Christmas present that first year when we had no idea what else to give them.

Along toward Christmas time they began to wonder what Christmas would be like without any money or toys or Christmas dinner. We promised them that with Christmas trees growing at our very door, rose hips and snowberries to make chains, they would remember this as the happiest Christmas of their lives. As a matter of fact, friends sent many gifts for the boys so they would have had something in any case.

On Christmas Eve we took the boys up to the study cabin to spend the night. We built a fire for them and left them tucked up in that solitary place, feeling a little timid, I think, though they wouldn't say so. They were to come down next morning when they heard a whistle. They had a clock so they wouldn't get up too early.

Early next morning Farrar moved the Christmas tree up to the new cabin we had built. We built a huge fire in the fireplace, decorated the cabin with fir and cedar boughs, cones, moss, snowberries, great clusters of madrona berries

which lasted, that year, until after New Year. The cabin was beautiful. The bunks were made up, one on each side of the door. We had built the cabin with five sides so that the fireplace could be in one corner and still leave the cabin exactly divisible by two.

At seven we whistled for the boys and I went up the trail to meet them, blindfolded them, and led them about the brush for awhile, telling them they were going into a secret cave. At the door of the cabin we got down on hands and knees and crawled into the cave. We took off their blindfolds when they were seated on their own bench beside the fire.

The boys blinked at the light and color. "It's our cabin," shouted North. "Oh, Bobby, it's a cabin for us! See the bunks!"

It was the happiest Christmas of their lives.

From *Living High*

As newlyweds, June and Farrar Burn homesteaded Sentinel Island in Spieden Channel in the San Juan Islands in the 1920s. Complete novices, and with no money, on their first Christmas they ate nothing but boiled cod, three times a day, for many days. Inveterate wanderers, the couple soon went to Alaska, later setting out to walk across America with a new baby in a cart pulled by a donkey. After many other escapades exploring America, and another baby, the Burns returned to Bellingham in Puget Sound, where June began writing a column for the *Daily Herald*.

They bought land on Waldron Island, and moved there at the beginning of the Depression, returning to Bellingham two years later. June studied nutrition and agriculture at the University of Missouri, and taught in many places. They lived again on Waldron Island, always dreaming of eventually returning to Sentinel Island.

Snow

by Kit Gifford
Queen Charlotte Islands, B.C.

I am of two minds about this snow.
Half of me delights at splendour tossed
In swirling curtains over sky and sea;
At crystal acres duned and drifted deep
In diamonds; pluming cedars, sculpted pines,
Etched, angled alders, everything white rimmed
Against a gull-grey late December sky.

The other, mother, half chafes restlessly
At cold-confinement—shackles formed of ice
On bush and branch, on shrouded, folded bud.
It worries for the hungry deer and browse;
For puddle-ducks bereft of puddles now.
It frets for small cold birds and podded seeds,
And cocooned butterflies, and buried toads.

I am of two minds about this snow—
Rejoicing at the double-crystalled night,
And yet repeating old North Coast adage
With plumed breath: "Better Wet than White."

From *Tales from the Queen Charlotte Islands: Book 2*

Kit Gifford is a poet and long-time resident of the Queen Charlotte Islands. She spends her summers gardening in a remote area of the Charlottes; she winters in Hawaii.

Elaborate Lunches

by David Lewis
Port Hardy, B.C., 1933

There were no movie theatres in the Port Hardy of the 1930s. There were no pools or skating rinks, no amusement parks. The residents had to make their own fun, and for the most part, they did a pretty good job of it. The town's social and recreational heart during this period was the community hall. Work on the hall was begun in January of 1933 under the auspices of the local community club. It was located on market street, two blocks from the government wharf on a lot donated by one of the Goodacres. Much of the lumber that went into it came from a dismantled fish cannery on Sushartie Bay and was paid for with money obtained in the sale of a smaller building which had been used by the community club since 1925. The work, like all work in the young settlement, was done by the townspeople themselves. They laboured without pay, receiving instead vouchers at a rate of $3.00 a day which would

Even in Christmas cards, fashions change.

admit the bearer to hall dances. It took them just under five months to do the job. The inaugural dance was held on June 2, 1933. The admission was 25¢. From then on every major community event centred on the hall.

Holidays were important in this respect and virtually the whole town turned out to celebrate them. (Not a difficult task when you consider that the population was under 200.) [. . .] Each Christmas it had a tree, and a party. The music then, as always, was provided by local musicians. What money was needed to pay for these celebrations came from a form of fund raising which is now all but extinct: the box social. It worked like this . . .

The women of the town would each make a lunch, often a very elaborate one, for reasons which will become apparent later. Each lunch was then wrapped up like a birthday gift and auctioned off at a public gathering. The buyer on these occasions not only got the food but also the company of its creator at dinner. Needless to say, the desire of the town's young men to dine with the girl of their choice made for some fairly intense competition when it came down to bidding, and the price of a single package often rose above $100.00. Should the bidding be for some reason slower than usual, some of the settlement's older bachelors would sometimes conspire to make the auction a success by bidding casually on lunches known to have been made by the sweethearts of particular boys. The old men had no intention of buying, but the panic that this tactic caused among the young suitors frequently set off a bidding war guaranteed to send prices through the ceiling. On one occasion the total raised by the auction reached $3500.00. The surplus from the funds raised in this manner went to buy Christmas dinner and presents to brighten the holidays for those who dwelt in outlying areas.

From *Yesterday's Promises: A History of the District of Port Hardy*

Port Hardy on northern Vancouver Island has a safe anchorage. Lumber and fish could be easily loaded onto sailing ships and steamers, making it an important port. The first government wharf was destroyed by a storm in 1918. The wharf mentioned in this story was built in 1926 on the west side of the bay near a new road. Gradually most residents moved across the bay to where Port Hardy is now.

The Empress Hotel's Warm Christmas Scrumpy
(non-alcoholic)

2 1/2 cups apple juice

2 1/2 cups boiling water

5 tablespoons maple syrup

3 drops bitters

4 cinnamon sticks

4 slices each lemon and lime

ground nutmeg

Combine apple juice, water, maple syrup, bitters and cinnamon sticks in a large saucepan. Heat for a few minutes to preferred serving temperature and to allow flavours to blend. Do not boil.

Pour into 12-ounce glasses or mugs. Garnish each with a twist of lemon and lime. Sprinkle with nutmeg and add an additional cinnamon stick for garnish. Makes 4 servings.

Hint: *Use a coffee maker to keep Scrumpy warm.*

Victoria's Empress Hotel has been keeping Christmas since the hotel opened in 1908, when it was decorated with the city's largest Christmas tree and celebrated with a Christmas Eve Ball.

Soldiers at Dinner

by Kathy Hogan
Cohassett Beach, Washington, January 3, 1942

Have you had a soldier at dinner? If you haven't, you'd better go out and get one right away. You will never feel that this is your war unless you do. After you have gotten your soldier, and fed him, and talked to him, this will have become your war—and the soldier, the one you had to dinner, will be fighting it for you.

We didn't get our soldier until the evening of Christmas Day. Due to government business, my host was unable to be at home until eight o'clock. Most of the boys on this beach had been nobly fed by that time as guests of honor in our hundred homes. But my hostess was determined. "There must be some boy who hasn't had Christmas dinner," she insisted, and so her husband put on his things again, got out his car, and went off. "Bring all you can find," she called after him.

But he only brought one. He brought him in proudly, as one brings home a rare hunting trophy. "I tried dozens of 'em," said my host, "and they'd all been fed. So I drove down to the water's edge and found this fellow just coming off a watch. He's cold, and hungry, and everything else that you'd want in a soldier," and my host looked approvingly at the soldier as if he'd invented him.

He was a big young fellow. His nice brown eyes accepted with a glance of appreciation the crackling fire, the decorations of pine branches and cones, the yellow fringed tablecloth on the pine table. He took off his muffler and folded it up, put his coat on a hanger—you'd have thought it was London made, the way he handled it—washed his hands, and sat down.

Two red candles lighted our feast. We talked of trivial, comfortable things. Outside, the North Pacific roared and rattled as it does on a fine night. Sometimes we stopped talking to listen to it. We looked into each other's eyes and thought of landing parties, submarines, and other enemy deviltry under the stars. But no one mentioned these things.

Our soldier talked of soldiering and the new army. He hailed from the Middle West, and his eyes were big with the wonders of this new country. Up

U.S. soldiers decorate a tiny tree for Christmas in Seattle, Washington, 1941.

on Hood Canal, he said, a watchman for oyster beds had told the boys they could have all the oysters they wanted for stews. So they got all they needed, and milked a nearby cow for milk. And it was such a grand oyster stew that they tried it again the next day—and the next, always falling back on the same cow. At the end of the fourth day, the company received a bill from a farmer for $24 worth of milk, so the stews came to an end.

When they found themselves bedded down in one of our forests during a wind storm, many of the boys from the plains country suffered acute discomfort and confessed that they felt like bolting. It would be easier to face enemy fire than to stay in the forest during a wind storm, they said.

Most of the boys in his company were in their early twenties, our soldier said. But they had one old fellow of thirty-five. He came from Arkansas. He didn't like the army much. His wife had had a fine job back in Arkansas and he'd lived on the fat of the land. And he would have been living on the fat of the land until this day, if his wife hadn't arisen to the national emergency and gone herself to the draft board and said, "Come and get him." So they came and got him, and since that day he didn't mind telling the world he'd been cheated. "Such a big healthy girl . . . and then to lay down on the job like that," was the way he put it to his comrades.

At eleven o'clock, we let our soldier out the door. His natural good manners would permit him to dine at Windsor Palace without untoward incident. Our hearts were large with pride. When we heard the garden gate click, we closed the door. Somehow the candle light seemed dimmer. And yet, we have something we didn't have before—we have a soldier at the front. Our own personal soldier.

From *Cohassett Beach Chronicles: World War II in the Pacific Northwest*

Kathy Hogan's weekly column, "The Kitchen Critic," appeared in the *Grays Harbour Post* in Aberdeen, Washington for ten years, starting in December 1941. After three failed marriages—"I loved them all dearly, but couldn't live with 'em"—Ms. Hogan, born in 1890, was living quietly on Cohassett Beach when America entered the Second World War. Her columns covered everything from growing a Victory Garden to spring cleaning and fishing. She died at Cohassett Beach in 1973.

Island Concert

by Patricia Forbes
Lasqueti Island, B.C., 1948

December of 1948 was my first experience at participating in Lasqueti's traditional island Christmas party. For my pupils and me it was quite an undertaking. I was nineteen years old, in my first teaching position, and fresh from city living in Vancouver.

My one-room school at Tucker Bay housed the sixteen children in the primary class, grades one to four, so our contribution had to be geared to their abilities. We had basically two things to do: prepare about twenty minutes of the concert program and decorate the classroom for the party as our school also doubled as the community hall. The remainder of the concert was the responsibility of the senior class, grades five to nine from False Bay School.

Volunteers of the Columbia Coast Mission built the Church of the Good Shepherd on Lasqueti Island.

Songs were sung, poems memorized and skits practised in the weeks prior to the last day of school before the holiday, the night of the island's party. Decorations of all sorts were made for the room as well as for the tall Christmas tree. Finally the desks were pushed to the edge of the room, the wood heater stoked, the lamps of the coal oil and gas lamps polished and we were ready for the guests.

The concert, the first part of the evening's activities, went off without a hitch. No one seemed to mind that the angels' halos were a bit crooked or that little Johnny had forgotten one of his lines. The children were heartily applauded for their efforts.

Reverend Alan Greene of the Columbia Coast Mission was always a part of Lasqueti's Christmas. This year his arrival on the *John Antle* brought the children a special treat—he had with him a movie projector that could run off a car battery and several reels of short films geared to the children's interests. Many of the children had never been off Lasqueti and for most of them this was their first experience with moving pictures. The films had been chosen well, cartoons and animal shows. The children shrieked with delight at the antics of four little bear cubs frolicking together.

After the films came the refreshment hour. Coffee and cocoa had been brewed and the ladies had outdone themselves with the wonderful display of sandwiches, cakes, and cookies. Everybody tucked in with enthusiasm and no one seemed to notice that Reverend Greene had disappeared.

Just as the last crumbs had been cleaned up, the sound the children had been waiting for so patiently could be heard. "Ho, ho, ho, Merry Christmas everyone!" and into the room popped that jolly chap in the red suit, a well-disguised Reverend Greene.

The island's two women's clubs took turns organizing the Christmas tree part of the festivities. Early in November they started soliciting the businesses supplying Lasqueti's needs, Eaton's, Woodwards, Simpsons, Spencers and Union Steamships to name a few, for contributions of cash or goods. This supplemented the cash donations collected from the island residents. The proceeds went to purchase a gift for every child on the island. As Santa called out their names, each child received a gift and a bag of candies, which also included a much treasured Japanese orange.

Finally, it was time to go home. I don't think it was visions of sugar plums that danced in my pupils' heads that night—I'm sure it was the antics of those mischievous bear cubs they had witnessed coming from that marvellous moving picture machine!

This is a reminiscence of Patricia J.M. Forbes, who, as a child in 1940, spent a summer holiday on a Lasqueti Island farm. She returned every summer for ten years, and began teaching on the island in 1948, taking time off for marriage and children. Mrs. Forbes resumed teaching on Lasqueti and later in Coquitlam, B.C. until her retirement, when she returned to live on Lasqueti with her husband.

A Shopping Trip

by R. Bruce Scott
Kildonan, B.C., 1950

It would be difficult to imagine a series of adventures more hazardous or bizarre than those of Nelson and Mina Dunkin, and their two children, aged two and four, while returning from a Christmas shopping expedition down the Alberni Inlet in December 1950.

Only recently having established themselves in Kildonan, a small village twenty miles down the inlet, they were, as yet, comparatively inexperienced water-wise, and unfamiliar with the dangers of navigation—dangers that lurk even in the comparatively sheltered waters of the inlet.

So it was that just a few days before Christmas they blithely set out in their small gasboat, which Nelson used for commercial fishing in the inside waters of Barkley Sound, to do some Christmas shopping in Port Alberni, at the head of the inlet, taking their two small children with them.

After they had finished their shopping, they left Port Alberni late in the afternoon and headed down the inlet for Kildonan. By the time they reached Nahmint, halfway down the inlet, it was dark and blustery, so Nelson decided to anchor in the mouth of the river for the night. Early the next morning, although it was still raining, and blowing, they started out again. They had not gone far when the boat hit a deadhead, a water-logged log that floats perpendicularly with one end invisible just below the surface, the other resting on the bottom if the water is shallow, floating if it is deep. In this case the log was resting on the bottom, and try as he would, Nelson could not dislodge the boat, which was holed and stuck fast. Fortunately they were towing a skiff. They also carried life jackets. Fastening the life jackets on the children, Mina climbed into the skiff. Nelson handed the children to her, then threw a bundle of blankets into the skiff. These and a small black bag containing a Christmas cake which a friend had given them as a parting gift, and a loaf of fresh home-made bread, were all that they took with them.

Mina waited while Nelson searched the boat for something which he did not find, then, seeing that the boat was about to sink, called to him,

"You'd better jump off." With no time to lose, Nelson took an axe, cut the rope that tied the skiff to the boat, and clambered in just as the gasboat sank beneath him.

Not knowing what to do, or where to go, they landed on the nearby shore. It was pouring with rain and the wind was still blustery. Remembering that there were some deserted Indian shacks farther up the river, Nelson decided to row there in search of shelter. By this time they, and the blankets, were soaking wet. Choosing the least dilapidated looking of the shacks, he lit a fire on the earth floor and tried to dry the blankets. It was obvious that they could go no farther in their twelve-foot skiff until the weather improved, so they prepared to spend the approaching night where they were.

Intending to serve a piece of Christmas cake to each before they turned in for the night, Mina opened the black bag and found that both the cake and the bread were soaked with saltwater and quite inedible.

Nelson found an empty fishbox (a strongly built box measuring three feet by two feet, used for packing fish for transportation to market) in the shack, so, turning it open side up, he lined it with blankets and used it as a cot for the children.

Sleep was out of the question. They tried to rest, but the roof leaked and the shack was filled with smoke from the fire, which they had to keep burning for warmth. The children cried restlessly. Nelson and Mina spent most of the night standing in the doorway to clear their eyes of smoke. They couldn't go outside because of the pouring rain.

When daylight came they were a sorry sight. Their faces were blackened by smoke, and their eyes red and sore. As Mina said, they looked just like smoked salmon.

"There's another shack farther up the river on the other side," said Nelson. "The Boy Scouts are building it for their summer camp. Let's go and try that one, it should be in better condition than this one."

They all clambered into the skiff and Nelson rowed upstream to the site of the Scouts' camp. On arrival, they found that it was still unfinished and only partly roofed. It had a shed roof and there were two rough bunks under the eaves. Disappointed at what they saw, they had no option but to stay the night and hope for the best. But it wasn't any better than the previous place. They lit a fire and it smoked copiously, billows of smoke filling the shack unbearably. They had to contend not only with smoke, but, as before, with a leaky roof; rain

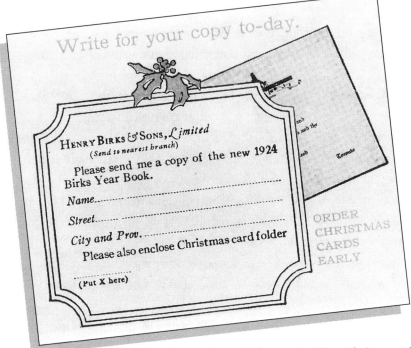

In coastal communities, Christmas shopping mostly meant catalogue shopping.

dripped through the roof and soaked them all thoroughly. They spent another sleepless night and, to add to their worries, the rain-swollen river flooded its banks and inundated the valley. All night long they heard the roar of rocks, loosened by the heavy rain, which thundered down the cliffs of the ravine—never knowing when one might roll on them. "It was just like thunder," Mina said, "just like thunder all night long."

When daylight came, Nelson saw an old Indian dugout canoe that had been partly chopped up, apparently for kindling. Both sides had been chopped halfway down. Nelson figured that it could be made serviceable by stuffing the cracks with rags, but where to find rags in that isolated place? His wife's dress, of course! They used the canoe as a dingy and stowed what few possessions they had in it in order to lighten the load in the skiff.

At long last the storm abated and the day became really calm. Knowing that there was a logging camp farther down the inlet at Long Bay, Nelson decided to head for it and stay there for the next night. Once more they set out. It was hard work rowing a skiff-load of humanity and towing a heavy dugout canoe, and it took a long time to cover even a short distance. As they emerged from the mouth of the Nahmint River into the Alberni Inlet, they saw a fishing boat coming down the inlet from Port Alberni. Nelson tied his white shirt to an oar and, standing up in the skiff, waved it vigorously to attract the attention of the boat owner. "He flagged that boat, and he flagged it, and flagged it," said Mina, "but it never changed course. We'll never know whether he saw us or not. Surely there had to be a reason! Anyway he went right on by."

Finally, after long hours of rowing, sometimes against the tide in the eddies that whirled along the shoreline, sometimes with it, sometimes with the wind, sometimes against it, they eventually arrived at Grumbach's logging camp at Long Bay. The place was in darkness and there was no sign of life when they knocked at the door. There was no response, so, leaving Mina and the children at the front door, Nelson went around to the back to see if there was any unlocked door or window that they could enter and take shelter for the night. While he was away the door suddenly opened and a tall man stood in the doorway and asked sullenly, "Well, what do you want? What are you doing here?"

Hearing the sound of voices, Nelson returned and told the man what had happened and that they would like shelter for the night. At first he refused, then seeing their bedraggled condition, reluctantly let them in. Cold, wet and hungry, not having eaten since their boat sank, Mina asked if they could get something to eat. At this he hummed and hawed. In desperation, Mina assured him that they knew the Grumbachs, owners of the camp, very well and felt sure that they wouldn't mind if she had a look around to see what she could find in the way of food. So he relented and told them to go ahead.

While the Dunkins rummaged for food, the man—apparently the caretaker—seated himself in an armchair with two cases of beer and two jugs of wine within arm's reach. "He had a wonderful time," said Mina. "He was a Swede, at least six feet tall. Obviously he had been drinking before we came, so he carried on where he had left off."

She did not say what they found to eat but they did find something and, while they were drinking their tea at the end of the meal, the man started swearing at them. He said he was a communist and launched into a long diatribe about what they were going to do to the capitalists in this country when the opportunity arose. The Dunkins suffered his outburst in silence then, in order to quiet him, said it was time for them to go to bed. But the man would not let them go. He continued the harangue. Finally, around ten o'clock, he told them they could go over to the bunkhouse to sleep.

"But do you know what he did?" asked Mina. "He told us to get up, then he lined us up in order with the smallest child first and Nelson at the end. He stuck a rifle in Nelson's back and said threateningly, 'Go on! March down to the bunkhouse!' Can you imagine? The stupid man! But we had to do what he said, so we walked over to the bunkhouse and when we got there he was reluctant to let us go. He didn't want Nelson to stay with me and the children, so he lined us up again and marched us back to the camp. There I laid blankets on the kitchen floor in front of the stove and we all lay down to rest. At two o'clock in the morning I heard a rustling noise. Looking up I saw this man in the doorway. He was looking into the kitchen where we were sleeping, and then he picked up his rifle off the floor. I jumped up and asked him what he was doing. 'Oh,' he said, 'I'm just going to look for the Grumbachs' dog; he might bite you.' With that he disappeared but, of course, we didn't sleep much that night."

As soon as daylight came the Dunkins arose, determined to get out of there as soon as possible, regardless of what might happen. Loading their few possessions into the dilapidated dugout canoe, they climbed into the skiff and cast off. By the time they reached Hell's Gate, a notoriously rough stretch of water where the wind funnels between steep cliffs, the wind had risen and there were whitecaps. Desperately Nelson headed for shore, but before he could make it the boat swamped and sank beneath them, leaving them all bobbing on the whitecapped waters.

"I don't know how long we were in the water," Mina related afterwards. "I had been sitting in the stern of the skiff with Madge on my knee. When the boat sank, I lost sight of Nelson and the boy. Fortunately the children had their life jackets on. Presently Nelson swam over to me and said 'Grab the canoe!' So I placed one arm over the gunwale and held on. Nelson lifted the boy into the canoe first, then he got Madge up and then he struggled to get me in, but he couldn't. I was too heavy. He got in himself and grabbed me and tried to haul me in that way. I was part way in when a wave washed me out again. Nelson caught me by the leg and held on until he could pull me in again. And, do you know? You'll never believe what happened! The canoe had been tied to the rowboat, but when the rowboat sank, Nelson had to let go the oars to grab the boy. The oars drifted away and we thought they had been lost, but do you know? When we got into the canoe, there were the oars in the canoe, just as if someone had placed them there! It was a miracle of God because it wasn't possible any other way!"

"Yes," Nelson added, "there was about six inches of water in the canoe, and there were the two oars floating inside the canoe." He shook his head in incredulity.

After bailing out the canoe, Nelson rowed behind Limestone Island for shelter. There, to their joy, they saw the familiar figure of Arthur Maynard, troll-fishing in the bay. Nelson rowed over to him and related briefly what had happened. Maynard invited them aboard and, after making them a hot cup of tea, took them home to Kildonan.

"That was our Christmas shopping expedition," said Mina. "I couldn't swim, neither could Nelson—not more than a few strokes. We can't but see God's marvellous help in that experience."

"Amen," added Nelson.

From *People of the Southwest Coast of Vancouver Island*

In 1903, the small Uchucklesit Cannery was opened in Alberni Inlet. The name was the Native word for "small spring at head of harbour." The cannery was renamed Kildonan by new owners in 1910. It changed hands several times before closing in 1960. The cannery was built on pilings over the ocean because that was the only flat "ground." The Dunkins lived in the area for many years before settling on Tzartus (Copper) Island, where they were the only residents.

The Holly

by Dudley H. Anderson
Victoria, B.C., 1913

Thou spirit, sweet that from the snow,
In green and purple all aglow,
Peeps forth so blithe and jolly,
We greet thee, spreading far and wide,
The joy, the pride of Christmastide,
We greet thee, radiant holly!

When trees and shrubs their branches bare,
Like warning fingers point in air,
As though they spoke the folly
Of putting on their garments gay
When winter blasts around them play,
Then brightest beams the holly.

This little boy graces a 1920s card.

Thou art in love with winter cold,
His icy arms thy form enfold,
While blushes every berry;
And this thy song of love that flows,
As softly as the falling snows;
"To all a Christmas merry!"

From *The Western Methodist Recorder*, December 1915

The Western Methodist Recorder, renamed *The Western Recorder* in 1925 after the unification of the churches, was a monthly publication of the Methodist Church. The magazine, with stories, letters, poems and reports of church activities around the world, had one editor, Reverend John P. Hicks, for its forty-seven years of publication from 1899 to 1946.

Permissions

Every effort has been taken to trace the ownership of copyright material used in the text. The author and publisher welcome any information enabling them to rectify any reference or credit in subsequent editions.

"December 24th," p. 3, reprinted by permission of Elizabeth Bakewell.

"Friendly Overtures," p. 9, original material published by Arrowsmith Press, Ltd., Port Alberni, B.C., edited for this printing by the Alberni District Historical Society.

"A Different Christmas Eve," p. 11, courtesy of the Archives of the Anglican Provincial Synod of British Columbia and Yukon.

"The Southerner Comes to Grief," p. 20, courtesy of James A. Gibbs.

"A Surprise Package," p. 23, reprinted by permission of Pruett Publishing Co., Boulder, Colorado.

"A Snowy Wedding," p. 28, reprinted with permission of UBC Press, Vancouver, B.C., from *The Reminiscences of Doctor John Sebastian Helmcken*, edited by Dorothy Blakey Smith.

"A Foggy Christmas Eve," p. 32, courtesy of Paul Merrick.

"Christmas Crabs," p. 44, courtesy of Sam Simpson.

"Letter Home," p. 54, reprinted with permission of UBC Press, from *The Vancouver Island Letters of Edmund Hope Verney, 1862–1865*.

"Brass Buttons," p. 59, reprinted with permission of the Agassiz and Harrison Historical Society.

"Holiday Travel," p. 60, courtesy of the Alberni District Historical Society.

"Laddie," p. 62, reprinted by permission of Harbour Publishing, Madeira Park, B.C.

"Christmas Day on a War Ship," p. 69, courtesy of the United Church B.C. Conference Archives.

"Logger's Gastown Christmas," p. 74, courtesy of *The Vancouver Province*.

"The Logger's Winter," p. 79, courtesy of the Archives of the Anglican Provincial Synod of British Columbia and Yukon.

"Ice Cream for Christmas," p. 82, courtesy of the Campbell River and District Museum and Archives Society.

"Sunbeam," p. 84, courtesy of the United Church B.C. Conference Archives.

"A Surprise Guest," p. 87, reprinted with the permission of Ohio University Press/Swallow Press, Athens, Ohio, from *Klondike Women: True Tales of the 1897–98 Gold Rush*, by Melanie J. Mayer.

"Presents and Poker," p. 89, reprinted with permission of Harbour Publishing, Madeira Park, B.C.

"Christmas Ships Come Sailing In," p. 93, courtesy of Elisabeth Hakkinen.

"Christmas Visitor," p. 95, courtesy of the Haida Gwaii Museum at Qay'llnagaay.

"John Boots," p. 97, courtesy of the United Church B.C. Conference Archives.

"A Union Bay Christmas," p. 100, courtesy of Janette Glover Geidt.

"Christmas on Nelson," p. 105, courtesy of Karen Southern.

"A Savary Celebration," p. 108, courtesy of Gladys Bloomfield.

"Sorrow and Joy," p. 114, courtesy of the Archives of the Anglican Provincial Synod of British Columbia and Yukon.

"Christmas Cabin," p. 118, courtesy of Skye Burn.

"Snow," p. 120, courtesy of Kit Gifford.

"Soldiers at Dinner," p. 124, courtesy of Klancy Clark de Nevers and Lucy B. Hart.

"Island Concert," p. 127, courtesy of Patricia Forbes.

"A Shopping Trip," p. 130, courtesy of Susan Scott, with appreciation to R. Bruce Scott.

"The Holly," p. 136, courtesy of the United Church B.C. Conference Archives.

Text Sources

Andersen, Doris. *Evergreen Islands: The Islands of the Inside Passage, Quadra to Malcolm.* Sidney, B.C.: Gray's Publishing, 1979. pp. 59–61.

Anderson, Dudley H. "Holly," *The Western Methodist Recorder.* Vancouver, B.C. December 1915.

Antle, John. "Christmas on the Columbia," *The Log of the Columbia.* Vancouver, B.C. December 1931. p. 2.

Arctander, John William. *The Apostle of Alaska: The Story of William Duncan, of Metlakahtla.* New York: Fleming H. Revell Co., 1909. pp. 312–14.

Arima, Izo. "Four years at Ikeda Bay," *The Charlottes: A Journal of the Queen Charlotte Islands. Vol. 3.* Masset, B.C.: Queen Charlotte Islands Museum Society. pp. 25–26.

Backus, Harriet Fish. *Tomboy Bride.* Boulder, Col.: Pruett Press, 1969. pp. 145–48.

Bateman, Lillian Lamont. "Stories of Horseshoe Valley," *Forgotten Villages of the B.C. Coast.* Raincoast Chronicles, ed. Howard White. Madeira Park, B.C.: Harbour Publishing, 1987. pp. 8–9.

Bird, George Hubert. *Tse-wees-tah—one man in a boat.* Port Alberni, B.C.: Arrowsmith, 1972. pp. 44–45.

Bloomfield, Gladys. In Kennedy, Ian. *Sunny Sandy Savary.* Vancouver: Kennell Pub., 1992. pp. 97–98.

Burn, June. *Living High: An Unconventional Autobiography.* Friday Harbor, Wash.: Griffin Bay Book Store, 1992.

Carr, Emily. *The Book of Small.* Toronto: Clarke, Irwin, 1942. pp. 171–75.

Clarke, Katie Walker. "Christmas Memories—No one had much money," *Musings.* Campbell River, B.C.: Campbell River and District Museum and Archive Society, November 1984. p. 6.

Crosby, Thomas. "Our First Christmas among the Tsimpseans," *The Western Methodist Recorder.* Vancouver, B.C. December 1899. p. 5.

Dye, Eva Emery. *McLoughlin and Old Oregon: A Chronicle.* Chicago: A.C. McClure & Co., 1900. pp. 122–28.

Evans, Hubert. *Whittlings.* Madeira Park, B.C.: Harbour Publishing, 1976.

Fawcett, Edgar. *Some Reminiscences of Old Victoria.* Toronto: Briggs, 1912. pp. 156–57, 261–62.

Forbes, Patricia. "Christmas on Lasqueti 1948." Personal communication, February 1999.

Fraser, George. "The Logger's Winter," *The Log of the Columbia*. Vancouver, B.C. December 1906. p. 12.

Geidt, Janette Glover. *The Friendly Port: The History of Union Bay, 1880–1960*. Union Bay, B.C.: D.R. Geidt, 1990. pp. 284–85.

Gibbs, Jim. *Shipwrecks of the Pacific Coast*. Portland, Ore.: Binfords & Mort, 1962. pp. 11–13.

Gifford, Kit. "Snow," *Tales from the Queen Charlotte Islands: Book 2*. Masset, B.C.: Senior Citizens of the Queen Charlotte Islands, 1982. p. 74.

Goodfellow, Florence. *Memories of Pioneer Life in British Columbia*. Hope, B.C.: Canyon Press Ltd., 1982. p. 28.

Graham, Donald. *Keepers of the Light: A History of British Columbia's Lighthouses and Their Keepers*. Madeira Park, B.C.: Harbour Publishing, 1985. pp. 20–21.

Greene, Alan. "A Christmas Eve Story That is Different," *The Log of the Columbia*. Vancouver, B.C. December 1951. pp. 6–7.

Hakkinen, Elisabeth. "The Christmas Ships Visited Haines, Alaska in Days Gone By." Personal communication, March 1999.

"Heavy Mails Now the Rule." *The Province*. Vancouver, B.C. December 1901.

Helmcken, John Sebastian. *The Reminiscences of Doctor John Sebastian Helmcken*, ed. Dorothy Blakey Smith. Vancouver: UBC Press, in co-operation with the Provincial Archives of British Columbia, 1975. pp. 296–97.

Hicks, John P. "Christmas Day on a Warship," *The Methodist Recorder*. Vancouver, B.C. December 1901. pp. 3–4.

Hogan, Kathy. *Cohassett Beach Chronicles: World War II in the Pacific Northwest*, eds. Klancy Clark de Nevers and Lucy Hart. Corvallis, Ore.: Oregon State University Press, 1995. pp. 6–7.

Lewis, David. *Yesterday's Promises: A History of the District of Port Hardy*. Victoria, B.C.: Robinson Press, 1978. p. 30.

Mayer, Melanie J. *Klondike Women: True Tales of the 1897–98 Gold Rush*. Athens, Ohio: Swallow Press/Ohio University Press, 1989. pp. 124–26.

Moser, Charles. *Reminiscences of the West Coast of Vancouver Island*. Victoria, B.C.: Acme Press, 1926. pp. 148–49.

Peterson, Lester R. *The Cape Scott Story*. Langley, B.C.: Sunfire Publications, 1985. p. 101.

Roberts, L.H. *The Trail of Chack Chack*. New York: Carlton, 1968. pp. 144–53.

Scott, R. Bruce. *People of the Southwest Coast of Vancouver Island: A History of the Southwest Coast*. Victoria, B.C.: R.B. Scott, 1974. pp. 107–12.

Sheepshanks, John. *A Bishop in the Rough*. London: Smith, Elder, 1909. pp. 26–27.

Simpson, Sam L. "Adventures in the Crab Trade." *Tales from the Queen Charlotte Islands: Book 2*. Masset, B.C.: Senior Citizens of the Queen Charlotte Islands, 1982. pp. 90–92.

Southern, Karen. *The Nelson Island Story*. Surrey, B.C.: Hancock House, 1987. pp. 180–82.

Swan, James Gilchrist. *The Northwest Coast; or, Three years' residence in Washington Territory*. Seattle: University of Washington Press, 1972. pp. 325–26.

Tate, C.M. "How John Boots Helped the Christmas Feast," *The Western Methodist Recorder*. Vancouver, B.C. December 1902. pp. 7–8.

Taylor, Charlie, Sr. Interview by Ed Cox (in Pioneer Parade). "Christmas Celebrations," CJAV Radio, Port Alberni, B.C. Unpublished. December 1946.

Tickner, Florence. *Fish Hooks & Caulk Boots*. Raincoast Chronicles 14. Madeira Park, B.C.: Harbour Publishing, 1992. pp. 40–41.

Tulloch, James Francis. *The James Francis Tulloch Diary: 1875–1910*, ed. Gordon Keith. Portland, Ore.: Binford & Mort, 1978. p. 16.

Verney, Edmund Hope. *The Vancouver Island Letters of Edmund Hope Verney, 1862–1865*, ed. Allan Pritchard. Vancouver, B.C.: UBC Press, 1996. p. 182.

Walkem, W. Wymond. "Stories of Early British Columbia." Vancouver, B.C. *News-Advertiser*, 1914. pp. 87–94.